I CAN TAKE IT FROM HERE

*A Memoir of Trauma, Prison,
and Self-Empowerment*

LISA FORBES

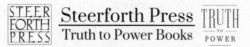
STEER FORTH PRESS · Steerforth Press · Truth to Power Books · TRUTH TO POWER

LEBANON, NEW HAMPSHIRE

For information about permission to reproduce
selections from this book, write to:
Steerforth Press L.L.C., 31 Hanover Street, Suite 1,
Lebanon, New Hampshire 03766

In 2020, Steerforth Press launched Truth to Power Books: investigative journalism,
iconoclastic histories, and personal accounts that are nuanced, thoughtful, and reliable
— qualities at a premium in the Internet age — and that inform through storytelling,
not argument.

Cataloging-in-Publication Data is available from the Library of Congress

ISBN 978-1-58642-304-9 (Paperback)

Manufactured in the United States of America

1 3 5 7 9 10 8 6 4 2

AUTHOR'S NOTE

It is an under-recognized fact that most former prisoners in the United States are traumatized before entering prison or while in prison. Many published studies indicate that most incarcerated people experienced childhood abuse or neglect.

In 2016, the American Psychological Association published an article that asserted, "Nearly all youth detained in the juvenile justice system have experienced traumatic events often leading to Post-Traumatic Stress Disorder." These boys and girls will "remain at risk for future offending" unless they receive treatment for PTSD and associated conditions. Many of those traumatized youth end up in adult prisons, just as I did.

According to the United States Department of Justice, more than 650,000 ex-offenders, or people I prefer to call restored citizens, are released from prison every year, and studies show that approximately two-thirds will likely be rearrested within three years of release. As a society, we will never end mass incarceration and mass recidivism until we acknowledge and address the role trauma plays alongside other factors, such as systemic racism and poverty.

The book that follows is my story, but in many ways it is also the story of millions of other individuals, and part of the story of our nation. We are all in this together.

CONTENTS

ESCAPE

For a long time, I thought I would get out of prison. I was confident a judge would overturn my sentence on appeal and free me to raise my young daughter. I was a nineteen-year-old Black girl from the projects and the people who judged me, mostly white men and a few senior citizens, one of whom the bailiff had to prod repeatedly for sleeping during my murder trial, were hardly a jury of my peers.

Guilty, they had said.

"Don't worry," my state-appointed appellate public defender had assured me.

The state of Illinois sent me to the Dwight Correctional Center in 1987. A lot happened that year. The stock market crashed, Michael Jackson released *Bad*, the dusky seaside sparrow became extinct, Jesse Jackson ran for president, Eli Lilly pitched Prozac to a jittery nation, and a jury convicted me of murdering James Bankston. The state of Illinois moved me from the Cook County Jail — where I had languished for eighteen months awaiting trial — to Dwight, a maximum-security women's prison some seventy miles from Chicago. A sickeningly cheerful security guard gave me a baggy blue uniform. I got a prison number, too: N77122. In prison, the women played Scrabble, took antidepressants, and watched *Cops*. At night, I dreamed I was in a different place, back home with my daughter.

My parents, who visited me once a month, thought I would get out, too, although we rarely discussed my appeal. Instead, we talked about politics, home, and religion. My mother brought me *Watchtower* and *Awake!* magazines, jammed with stories about missionaries, earthquakes, and the end of the world. Soon, the authors said, natural disasters would plague mankind no more. "Under God's Kingdom, every tear of sorrow will be wiped away forever."

My father, who grew up in Jackson, Tennessee, often talked about the South, and shared memories of his family. He didn't like the boys who dated his sisters. Once, a mule kicked an unlucky relative in the head and, he said, "he was never the same after that."

My father loved city politics. He talked about Harold Washington, the first Black mayor of Chicago. Washington died unexpectedly in 1987, shortly after I'd gotten to Dwight, and two Black men — Timothy Evans and Eugene Sawyer — vied for his job. Evans gained the support of African American voters, who saw Sawyer as a puppet. But Sawyer, supported by a mix of white and Black voters, won. Worried about protesters, Sawyer was sworn in at 4:01 A.M. in the parking lot of a closed restaurant. It was the talk of the town.

My mother, a Jehovah's Witness, pooh-poohed such talk. City councils, school committees, presidential candidates — flawed rulers could not change the world. She said, "There's no solution to any of these worldly problems except in Jehovah's Kingdom."

My daughter, Mercedes, sat on my lap, looked around, and played happily as we talked. My mother dressed her in a pretty blouse; her hair was always full of barrettes. But she wasn't worry-free.

Three years later, in 1990, I was still waiting for my appeal to be heard. Mercedes had just started first grade. Almost seven, she was a bright little girl and a budding writer. She loved to write short stories. My mother mailed copies of them to me. Full of three-dimensional characters, they included amazing, complex plots. But they weren't fairy tales with happy endings. Her characters tended to be sad or angry. I wondered if her stories reflected some inner anguish.

When I told my parents about my concerns, my mother laughed, shook her head, and said, "They're just stories."

Mercedes favored her father: light complexion, curly hair, brown eyes. "Is she Puerto Rican?" people asked. By the time I went to prison, she had only seen her father a few times. I don't think she connected his absence to my incarceration. I never talked about my crime. How do you explain a twenty-five-year sentence to a little girl who falls asleep clutching a Cabbage Patch doll — a doll that her father gave her? How do you tell your daughter you murdered her father?

During these visits, I tried hard not to cry, but usually I did. Occasionally Mercedes asked when I was coming home. I always smiled and said, "Soon."

It could have been worse, several inmates told me. Some killers spend a lifetime behind bars. I might get out in my thirties. I wasn't comforted. My life in Chicago's public housing projects had been awful enough. At four, I was hit by a car. An older brother sexually molested me for years, my sisters bullied me, my father drank, and my mother talked about "the last days." God would destroy the world's nonbelievers, she said, including me. "Jehovah knows who he's going to kill."

Jehovah would have to get in line. I was so miserable, I thought about killing myself every day. We lived on the sixth floor of a sixteen-story high-rise in a sea of public housing. I wanted to jump from a high window and leave my unhappy life behind. My daughter saved me from that fate. I named her Mercedes, not after the car, but after Our Lady of Mercy. I understood her to be the patron saint of abuse victims, incest victims, and martyrs, but I wasn't Catholic, and I may have gotten her mixed up with other caring saints. After I went to jail, I learned she was the patron saint of prisoners, too. All I knew was that my daughter was my lifeline. Her unconditional love sustained me like an umbilical cord whose connections were reversed.

Prison mangled that bond. "Sometimes she cries at night," my mother told me on one visit. "She won't stop. She cries and says, 'I want my mama.' I tell her, 'Your mama's not here,' and she cries herself to sleep."

In the fall of 1990, I got a letter from the appellate court during mail call. Realizing a lawyer would have called if the news was good, my heart sank. I tore open the manila envelope. The court had decided to uphold my conviction. Back in my room, I sat on my bunk, too stunned to cry. Two days later, Mercedes turned seven.

That's when I decided to break out.

I continued to meet with my family each month, but our visits served a new purpose: I used them to plot my escape. Every month we met in the visitors room, a large space with folding chairs at various tables. Visits were limited to four hours. The room was noisy, crowded — sometimes I waited an hour for a table — and someone was always crying. Visitors and inmates bought candy, crackers, and chips from the vending machines on one wall. Or they ordered pizzas, hot sandwiches, and ice cream at a deli-style counter. The correctional officers, or COs, sat behind a glass enclosure to the right of the counter. The room included a row of monitors tied to cameras trained on every part of the security fence. I paid careful attention to these cameras on visitation days. Waiting in line for pizza or an Italian beef sandwich, I held Mercedes in my arms, made small talk with my parents, and studied the screens. A few, no longer working, had gone dark. They were the prison's blind spots.

I studied the layout of my new home in earnest. Established in 1930 as the Oakdale Reformatory for Women, the renamed Dwight Correctional Center was overcrowded, understaffed, and underfunded in the late 1980s. It didn't even have a chapel — just a few Bible study classes. More than half of the prisoners took psychotropic drugs that kept them drowsy. The women who had been addicted on the streets to crack or heroin were now addicted in prison to Elavil, Sinequan, and Adapin — mood-altering drugs that were dispensed as readily as breath mints to help the women deal with "depression."

Although the inmates were young, mostly in their twenties and thirties, many of them had few teeth or wore dentures, either because drugs had rotted their teeth or because someone had knocked them out. The ones convicted of murder had killed their husbands, boyfriends, or tricks. A few had killed their babies or children. But women were also serving hard time for being petty thieves or "boosters," stealing and reselling clothes and jewelry.

Every one of us, I'm quite certain, struggled with acute trauma tied to physical, sexual, or emotional abuse.

We all wore colored ID cards to indicate our flight risk. An ID card with a white background signified a low risk. After that, the ranking was blue, medium risk; red, high risk; and green, extremely high risk. Except for a few women who had escaped from work release centers, nearly every inmate wore a white badge. Nobody dreamed of running. Those with children talked about their children. Those about to be released imagined their lives on the outside. Most of the women had forged lesbian relationships and prison "families." They had a wife, a husband, and a younger inmate who was their son or daughter, or an older inmate who was their momma. The inmates were their family, and the prison was their world. Dwight treated their inner pain with tranquilizers.

We lived in cottages, not cell blocks — stone houses with steel and glass front doors. I slept in a medium-security cottage, C-14. My cell had a door with a small window. The guards could oversee the dayrooms in each building through a glass enclosure in the middle. The women passed the time watching their favorite TV show, *Cops*. Every day the theme song filled the dayroom: "Bad boys, bad boys, whatcha gonna do? Whatcha gonna do when they come for you?"

I could not understand why anybody in prison would want to watch that show.

Like other minimum- and medium-security inmates, I was allowed to stroll along a gravel path that ran inside the prison fence. I simply needed to let the COs know that I was going for a walk. After my appeal was denied, I walked with a new purpose. I memorized the screens in the visitation room and looked for blind spots along the path. I spotted one between the wall and the Industry Building, where the "privileged" inmates sewed garments for Illinois prisoners, including handkerchiefs, blue pants, blue shirts, white shirts, pajamas, and dusters. They earned a dime a garment.

I planned my breakout to take place during evening recreation. The rec yard was a grassy area inside a four-foot-tall chain-link fence, a prison within a prison. It featured picnic benches, a volley-ball net, a walking trail, and a snack shack where inmates could buy two-ounce packets of Carl Buddig meats (beef, turkey, and honey ham), pizza, Italian beef sandwiches, chips, soda, and ice cream. We could eat in the rec yard or take food and soda back to our cottages. We could bring a radio (the prison commissary sold boom boxes) or wear a Walkman in the yard. We could also take cards or a board game and play bid whist, pinochle, Uno, or Scrabble.

When I went to the rec yard, I usually took a book. I was teaching myself Spanish so I could talk to some of the other inmates, so I often carried a Spanish-English dictionary with me. My plan was simple: Walk the road, duck behind the Industry Building, find the blind spot, and climb the fence. I waited a few weeks to make sure no one repaired the monitors. And I walked the road several nights a week to make sure the number of people on the path didn't change on different days. I had no plan beyond climbing the fence, running into the woods, and calling someone to get me.

Evening rec was two hours long. The guards spent another hour counting the returning prisoners. It would be at least three hours before anyone noticed I was missing. Plenty of time to get lost.

On the day of the break, I put on sneakers and a gray, long-sleeved jogging suit. I carried a button-down jean jacket to throw over the barbed wire once I topped the fence. I had purchased the clothes from the commissary. Those who couldn't afford new clothes wore the standard navy-blue prison uniform with a matching, shapeless blue prison jacket.

I got in the rec line with everyone else and filed out. Most of the COs stood around in the yard. A single car rolled along the path. Two or three COs walked the route, but they were spaced pretty far apart. At a casual pace, it took about forty minutes to complete the circuit. But the COs almost always stopped to talk to inmates, giving me more time. I knew that once I passed a CO, I could go at least ten minutes without seeing another one. The patrol car moved slowly, too. I'd have more than enough time. Plus, I had the advantage of surprise.

One thing worried me: What if I encountered another inmate on the path? They might blow the whistle on me. Or they might just join me on the walk and be chatty. How could I get rid of them without drawing attention to myself? I didn't want to do anything that might appear unusual.

I had nothing to worry about. The road was empty that day. It was near dusk on a crisp November evening — pleasant enough to huddle together in the rec yard but too chilly to go for a stroll. The rec yard was crowded, the inmates were content, and the COs were in a friendly and relaxed mood. I walked casually toward the Industry Building and faced the fence in the blind spot. No one saw me. I had no plan beyond getting on the other side of the fence, but I felt no fear, and I wasn't worried. I was drawn to the fence like a moth to a flame. Without hesitation, I put a foot on the fence and pulled myself up. Climbing the chain link was easy. The wide razor wire at the top presented the challenge. It tore my jacket, sliced through my palms and thumbs, slashed the knuckle of my left ring finger down to the bone, and plucked circular plugs of flesh from my forearms.

I pressed on.

Then, at the top of the fence, I panicked. The razor cut into my left thigh. It stretched before me for three feet — much wider than it looked from the ground. I couldn't just swing my legs over it and climb down. The barbs nibbled at my forearms like flesh-eating piranhas. I flailed wildly in a futile effort to keep my arms free as my useless jacket became entangled in the wire.

I lost my balance and fell backward — a fifteen-foot drop — landing hard on my back inside the prison. The breath whooshed from my body. I tried to stand but collapsed immediately. My left ankle, broken, bulged to the right and over the top of my sneaker. I stared at it, oddly calm. Blood ran from my hands and dampened my jogging suit. I wasn't going to climb a fence with a shattered ankle, and I needed medical attention. Lying on my right side, I dragged myself to the road where I could be seen and sat on the ground in front of the Industry Building. I cradled my ankle and held it in place.

Looking up, I could see the November sky, the prison lights, and the bloodied razor wire above me.

I was going nowhere.

book one

Chicago

JUMP

Other girls in my neighborhood played with dolls and jumped double dutch. I wanted to kill myself. I spent a lot of time standing at the windows in our sixth-floor apartment. My parents and siblings — if they thought about me at all — probably thought I was looking at the street below.

Not that there was much to see. Some run-down houses across the street. A couple of small stores selling high-priced junk food to people with no money to spare. A vacant lot filled with drunks — my father included — leaning on cars and talking loudly about nothing. Everywhere, people walked slowly, going nowhere. The view was a little better from my bedroom window, but not by much. I could see the city bus after it turned the corner. At least people seemed to be going somewhere, getting off, going home, catching other buses. I could see another vacant lot. And I could see the second of the three sixteen-story buildings in the public housing complex where we lived.

I wanted to jump from all those windows.

For the next nine years, I felt lost, angry, and depressed. I could have run away, but where would I go? Who would believe my story? Outsiders thought we were a godly household. We were, after all, Jehovah's Witnesses. Every Sunday, we dressed up and walked to the nearby Kingdom Hall, a red-brick single-story building with no windows on 42nd Street in Chicago. There were no wooden pews, just folding chairs set up by teenage volunteers before the meetings. The chairs faced a stage and podium. The disfellowshipped people — former Witnesses hoping to get reinstated — sat in the back and could speak only to the elders. A person could be thrown out of

the congregation for several reasons, including disagreeing with
the doctrine as put forth by the Watchtower Bible and Tract
Society, smoking, or fornication. The disfellowshipped were
outcasts, shunned by family and friends. They lived on the outside,
looking in.

On weekdays we studied the Bible, sometimes in our neighbors'
apartments. We tried to bring as many people as possible into "the
Truth." On Saturday mornings, instead of sleeping late or watching
cartoons, we got up early, put on our good clothes (dresses, skirts,
and blouses for girls; shirts, ties, and jackets for boys), and met
other Witnesses, or "friends," at Kingdom Hall. The elders assigned
us our territories. For hours we knocked on doors, sold or handed
out *Awake!* and *Watchtower* magazines, and told strangers about
Jehovah, Armageddon, and the end of the world.

At the Kingdom Hall, we got advice on how to "deliver the
message" about God's plan. My mother made us practice what we
were going to say. One tactic was to get homeowners or renters to
answer yes to every question.

"You have a name, don't you?" we asked.

"Yes."

"And everybody that you know has a name, don't they?"

"Yes."

"And people should be called by their name, shouldn't they?"

"Yes."

"Well, if you can agree that you have a name, and you can agree
that everybody you know has a name, and you can agree that
people should be called by their name, then why can't you agree
that, if the Bible says that God has a name and His name is Jehovah,
everybody should call Him by that name?"

That was our opening, our foot in the door.

"Let me show you in the Bible where it says that God's name is
Jehovah," we said. We pointed to Psalms 83:18 and read, "That men

may know that you, whose name alone is JEHOVAH, art the most high over all the earth."

The religious tracts we handed strangers asked lots of questions. *What are your hopes for the future? Do you just want to live out a few years on earth with the hope of gaining some pleasure and happiness before you die? What hope have you of life after death? What does the future hold for mankind in general? Will some disaster finally destroy the earth and all life on it?*

We had a calling. Each month we turned in a time card tallying the hours we spent in the field, spreading Jehovah's word. One blustery, snowy day, my mother hauled me outside in field service with her. A man carrying groceries trudged by and said, "Dragging them kids out in this weather." My mother didn't respond. But after we passed him, she told me, "I'd rather do this than die like a dog in the street!"

That's what she thought would happen to her if she didn't do what the "elders" and "the Society" — folks gathered in the Jehovah's Witnesses headquarters in Brooklyn — demanded. Armageddon would come, and Jehovah would kill her like a dog in the street.

It sure seemed like we were God-fearing folks who simply wanted to help everyone discover "the Truth" before it was too late. We didn't socialize with worldly people. We didn't fornicate or hang Christmas stockings or open birthday presents. We were different — better, somehow. And we were good people, right? Especially the mother, who knocked on doors in the snow.

So why did I want to die while other little girls played with dolls in their bedrooms?

FRIENDLY GHOSTS

I cried when my older sisters and brothers left for school. It was 1969. I was three. We hadn't yet moved into the high-rise on Lake Park Avenue. We lived in a three-story apartment building at 6405 South Ellis Avenue on the South Side of Chicago. We had a porch, a backyard, and a dog named Frisky. Sobbing, I watched my sisters and brothers leave for school. The youngest of six, I had to stay behind. My mother led me away from the living room window and into the dining room. We sat at a table and played school.

From that point on, we played school every weekday morning. I studied the children's books my older siblings had tossed aside. I learned the alphabet and how to sound out words phonetically. We had a lot of Dr. Seuss's books, *The Cat in the Hat* and *Green Eggs and Ham*. "The sun . . . did not . . . shine," I read slowly. "So we sat . . . in the house . . . all that cold, cold, wet day." Practice, my mother said. Sound out the words. She was calm, patient, deliberative. She never yelled. My brother Kirk taught me how to spell the word *arithmetic*. "Just remember the first letters of every word in this sentence," he said. "A rat in the house may eat the ice cream." A-R-I-T-H-M-E-T-I-C.

One day a neighbor's child stopped by to borrow some sugar. She was eleven or twelve years old. My mother let her in and led her to the kitchen. I sat in the dining room reading. The girl stopped and stared at me. "Is she reading for real?" she asked. When my mother said yes, she burst into tears. My mother comforted her and told her that she, too, could learn to read. She just needed someone to teach her. The little girl left with the sugar, still crying.

I sucked a bottle until I was three. I drank cold milk like every-one else at home, but I poured mine into a bottle instead of a glass. I always went to sleep with my bottle. Every morning, right after I woke up, I walked into the kitchen and put the empty bottle on the floor. I grabbed the carton of milk from the refrigerator and poured some of it into the bottle. Everyone else drank from cups and glasses. Not me. I walked around with a bottle I had fixed myself. One morning I couldn't find it. I asked my mother where my bottle was. She and one of my sisters told me that Casper the Friendly Ghost had taken it. Since I liked the Casper show, and watched him every day on TV, I didn't mind him having it. The cartoon Casper wasn't scary. He didn't haunt houses. Mostly he wanted to play and make friends. I stopped drinking from a bottle after that.

My world changed the day my mother became a Jehovah's Witness. I remember her sitting at the kitchen table with a man who read the *Watchtower* magazine with her. He always wore a suit. I remember him smiling. My mother became very serious about life. From that time forward, she was sure the world would end. "Armageddon could start any minute now." We stopped cele-brating Easter, Halloween, Thanksgiving, and Christmas. I had no cake or candles on my fourth birthday. My world got smaller, too. We couldn't have friends over because they weren't Witnesses. "Bad associations spoil useful habits," my mother said, quoting First Corinthians 15:33 from the Bible. She started talking about how Jehovah didn't like it when we were disobedient. We shouldn't be "hardheaded" because it was important to have a "good rela-tionship" with Jehovah, she said.

One morning my mother left home to go to the grocery store. My older sister Cheryl — the same one who told me that Casper took my bottle — was in charge of looking after me. We were all in the playground in the park across the street. Suddenly, I had to pee. I told my sister three times I needed to go.

"You gotta wait!" she told me. Each time, she turned her back on me to talk with her friends. Finally, I left the playground and headed to our apartment across the street. A big brown dog sat on the building's front porch. I was afraid it would bite me. I ran across the street to the building, but when the dog turned and looked at me, I ran back. I did that a couple of times. On my third try, a car hit me.

The blow knocked me unconscious. At the emergency room, a doctor treated my scrapes and bruises and stitched up my head. When I came home, my parents put me in their bed. The woman who struck me came by and gave me a big teddy bear. My mother told her that I was all right.

When she left, my mother and my sister told me that it was my fault the car hit me because I was hardheaded and disobedient.

After the accident, a little white girl befriended me. I don't recall the first time I saw her, and I don't remember how I learned her name. One day she was simply there, and I was glad. I never believed that she was imaginary or that there was anything odd about her. Her sudden appearance never frightened me. Chrissy became my constant companion for a year.

One day my mother asked, "Who you talking to?"

"Chrissy," I said. I told her about my new friend.

My mother stared at me. "Chrissy isn't real," she said.

But she was real. Her blond hair, parted in the middle, ended in two pigtails. She wore a pink short-sleeved, knee-length dress with white ankle socks. She wore a gold buckle on her black shoes. I liked Chrissy much more than my sisters and brothers for one very good reason: She was always on my side. It didn't matter that no one else could see or hear her. I could, and she was always there. When my sisters and brothers played together in the backyard, I played and talked with Chrissy in the bedroom I shared with my sisters. I was never alone. When I started kindergarten, she walked with me to school. At the end of the school day, she was waiting for me. She was my one true friend, and she made me feel safer and less alone.

I was never punished for playing with Chrissy or insisting she was real. But nobody believed me, either. And nobody wondered why I started seeing and talking to a little white girl after I got hit by a car.

I was glad to have the company. Wadsworth Elementary School, on South Ellis Avenue, was two blocks from home. Along with my sisters and brothers, I had to walk past an abandoned building to get home from school. That building always scared me. A damp, foul air assaulted my nose when we walked by, and my brothers repeatedly told the tale of how one day they were walking by the building with one of their friends and a huge rat ran out, grabbed their friend, and dragged him screaming into the building. They said they never saw their friend again. Curiously, they even told this story to my mother — as if they really believed it. But my mother said that it couldn't be true, because there were no reports of missing children in the neighborhood.

One day I walked home by myself. I was fine until I got inside the apartment building. As I walked up the stairs, a man wearing sunglasses approached me from the opposite direction. He asked me if I wanted to go somewhere with him and get some candy. I looked up at him and said, "My mama told me not to go nowhere." I ran by him and into the apartment. I told my mother what happened, and she ran to the door and looked down the stairs to see if she could find the man who spoke to me. But he was gone. "You did the right thing," my mother said.

One night, when I was still four, I started walking in my sleep. Everyone else was asleep. I got out of bed and stood at the dining room table, the same table where my mother and I played school. Still asleep, I thumbed through some books, trying to decide which one I wanted to read. Suddenly the room started filling up with water. I thought I was going to drown. I knew I needed to get out. For some reason I thought I was in a basement — even though we didn't have a basement. I ran into the kitchen. It had a back door that led down a flight of steps into the backyard we shared with the other tenants. I tried to get out the door, but I couldn't open the chain. I started screaming, "Let me out!" I banged my fists on the door. Then my mother and my father came into the kitchen and must have woken me up. Slowly, dazed and confused, I realized the water was gone and that I had dreamed it all.

WIGGLING

One night, when I was sleeping in my parents' bed, I felt the sheets moving. I woke up and saw my father lying on top of my mother. I looked at what he was doing to my mother, and then I started doing the same thing to the mattress. I got all sweaty. I climbed out of bed, walked down the hallway, and got a towel to wipe the sweat off my face and neck. Then I climbed back into my parents' bed. I saw my mother lying on her back, underneath my father, gaping at me, wide-eyed. My father was still doing what he was doing and paying me no attention, so I went back to doing what I had been doing. I had my first climax and went back to sleep. I was three.

The next morning, I woke up and walked into the kitchen. My mother was cooking on the stove. She looked at me and said, "Lisa, you can't do everything you see somebody else doing." I knew exactly what she was talking about. I said, "Okay." And we never spoke of it again. After that, I masturbated myself to sleep every night. My siblings called it "wiggling." "Ma, Lisa wiggling again!" they yelled whenever they caught me in the act. My mother would spank me while everybody watched. I would cry and promise not to do it again.

But it was the only way I fell asleep, so I couldn't stop.

THE LAKE MICHIGAN HIGH-RISES

My father worked briefly as a grocery store security guard. After he lost that job, my mother told him that we needed to live someplace cheaper. In 1971, shortly before I turned five, we moved to 4155 South Lake Park Avenue, a public housing project on the South Side of Chicago.

We left our dog, Frisky, because we couldn't keep a dog in the projects. My mother treated Frisky like another child. She cooked his food, usually some kind of beef stew, on the stove. On days when she served us tomato soup and a baloney sandwich, she still cooked for Frisky. Sometimes my sisters and brothers would come home from school and say, "Ooh, Ma, that smells good! What you cooking?" "That's Frisky's food," my mother would say. "Y'all can grab a sandwich." Frisky didn't eat dog food, and he didn't play with other dogs. We left Frisky with one of Daddy's friends. Daddy rubbed his head and said good-bye. Frisky had been a loyal companion. Every night he slept on the floor by my father's side of the bed.

"No one else will cook food for Frisky, so he'll have to learn how to eat dog food," my mother said.

We piled into a truck driven by one of my father's friends: my father, Townsell, my mother, Annie Jane, and — in order of birth — my sister Cheryl, my brother Townsell, my brother Kirk, my sister Faye, and me, the youngest. It took a few more trips to move all our furniture. My oldest sibling, Annette (Net, for short), was married and living with her husband and two daughters.

I tried to stay close to my mother during the move, but she kept telling me to stay out of the way. I didn't know what to do or where to go. My mother seemed overwhelmed by everything that had to be done. I was overwhelmed by the sky-high buildings filled with hundreds of families.

The Lake Michigan High-Rises, built by the Chicago Housing Authority (CHA), had another fancy-sounding name — Lakefront Homes. But whenever anyone asked where we lived, we just said "CHA."

Constructed in 1962 and completed in 1963, they consisted of three sixteen-story buildings that formed a U-shaped complex located west of Lake Shore Drive, one of Chicago's busiest expressways.

Two playgrounds stood between the buildings. The walk to the shores of Lake Michigan took about ten minutes. In winter, the wind whipped between the buildings and the windchill fell below zero. It was cold to the bone.

Though the buildings were only ten years old, you wouldn't know it. The smell of urine was everywhere. People stood around watching other people come and go. The elevators were usually broken, which meant a six-flight climb for us. Some parents had to lug their children and their groceries up sixteen flights of stairs. And the stairwells were dark. People were always breaking the bulbs.

The lights in the elevators didn't always work, either. When the doors closed, everyone stood in the dark until they opened again. The doors got stuck, too. Trapped inside, we screamed and banged on the door until someone either pried them open or called the fire department. Sometimes they broke on our way back from the Kingdom Hall. We could hear other people in the building laughing at us. "Ah ha, the JEE-hovah Witnesses are stuck in the elevator again." Eventually, we got out. But the ordeal was always terrifying.

Ironically, the concrete walkways on each floor were called gangways. The gangways were not enclosed when we moved in. Eventually, city workers covered each floor with metal grating.

People said it was to stop the tenants from throwing things — and people — from the building. Several gangs operated in the different projects, including the Gangster Disciples and Black Disciples, the Vice Lords and the El Rukns.

Sometimes I babysat the two daughters of a young mother, a Jehovah's Witness who moved from the Lake Michigan High-Rises into another housing project — the notorious Robert Taylor Homes. One evening, after a shopping trip, she got into the elevator. A man got in with her and knifed her repeatedly. He stabbed her in the neck and threw her body down the elevator shaft.

The next day, after school, I found my mother in the living room, standing at the window, wide-eyed.

"Did you know that Rhonda Sanders got killed last night?"

I dropped my book bag and fell heavily on the couch.

"She got killed? What happened?"

"I don't know," my mother said. "They found her body in the elevator shaft."

I stood up, suddenly scared. I grabbed my book bag, walked into my bedroom, and finished my homework. I tried hard to push the murder away. But I thought about Rhonda every day. I worried about playing outside, walking to school. I felt like her fate was tied to mine — or mine to hers.

We lived in a cramped three-bedroom apartment with one bathroom. If you've ever seen the 1970s TV sitcom *Good Times*, you know the place. And if you've ever been in a porta potty, you've smelled it. My parents had one bedroom, my two brothers slept in a second bedroom, and I shared the third bedroom with two older sisters, who slept in separate twin beds. I slept on a fold-up rollaway bed by the door.

My oldest sister, Annette, married with two daughters, lived elsewhere. But one day she and her daughters moved into the third bedroom, too. That was the girls' room, no matter how many girls there were. "I been married three times and ain't *none* of them worked out!" Net cried, bitterly, as she carried boxes and bags of clothes into our already too-crowded apartment. I was unhappy to have even more people in our room. I already felt like I had no space — let alone privacy. Now six of us slept and dressed in the same bedroom. Worse, I really didn't know my sister. Annette was thirteen years older than me. When I was five, she was eighteen. We didn't grow up together. She was already married when I was still in kindergarten. Her two daughters, my nieces, were only a few years younger than me. I knew Net was my sister, but her moving in felt like a stranger was moving into the apartment.

Plus she smoked cigarettes. Throughout the day she stood in front of an open window, blowing cigarette smoke out so the apartment wouldn't smell like smoke.

One day when I was about eleven years old, Net and my mother were in the kitchen. Since they were cooking and talking, my mother had told Net that she could smoke a cigarette without standing at the window. I walked into the kitchen, and ashes from Net's cigarette dropped onto my right forearm. It burned me.

"Ouch!" I screamed, and then I cried. Both Net and Mama ignored me. I stood in a corner of the kitchen, crying bitterly for several minutes, staring at the burn on my arm, not knowing what to do for it. Eventually Net walked over to me.

"Let me see your arm," she said matter-of-factly.

I stretched out my arm and showed her the burn. When she saw that she had actually burned me, she said, "Oh, I'm sorry, I thought you were just crying for attention! I didn't realize you really had a burn." She told me to come with her to the bathroom so she could take care of it.

Only then did my mother show any interest in my suffering. As I walked past her with Net, on my way to the bathroom, Mama walked toward me and said, "Let me see."

She reached out for my arm.

I looked at her and thought, *Why are you only acting like you're*

*interested in my suffering after somebody else responds to it first? Net
is not my mother, you are! But as long as Net was willing to ignore
me, you will ignore me, too? You do not care about me!*

I snatched my arm away angrily. My mother looked at me as if
she couldn't stand me. I walked into the bathroom, where Net ran
cold water over my burn.

I never felt like I had an inch of my own. There was never enough
closet space, and things were always on the floor, even though we
tried to keep the room neat. If my mother and father argued, my
mother would wake me up in the middle of the night, tell me to
move over, and get into bed with me. I spent my childhood nights
hanging off the edge of a twin-size rollaway bed. We had a bit more
space once we got bunk beds. One night I rolled out of the top
bunk and screamed when I hit the floor. "What happened?" my
father asked, standing in the doorway to our room. "I fell out the
bed!" I cried. He looked at my mother, waiting for her to do something. "You all right?" my mother asked. "Uh-huh," I said sleepily.
"Okay then," my mother said. My parents went back to bed. My
sisters went back to sleep. The next day my father told me to stay in
bed. "Don't get up running around," he said. "You'll be all right."

We didn't have a dining room, so we ate our meals in two rooms.
There wasn't enough space in the kitchen, so we spread out into the
living room. Somebody was always sitting on the couch, holding
their plate in their lap while they ate. The living room included a
small black-and-white television and shelves full of religious
books. My father had his own chair, a padded rocker. We could sit
in it, but only if Daddy was elsewhere. If he walked into the living
room, we got up. My father had his private plate and cup, too.
When my mother cooked, she would always fix my father's plate
for him. To the rest of us, she would say, "Everybody come fix your
plate! Dinner's ready!" My father's plate was a silver-colored metal
pie pan; his cup was a sixteen-ounce tin measuring cup, usually
filled with iced tea or lemonade. My father ate anything my mother

cooked. He liked chitlins, but my mother wouldn't cook them. One of his favorite things to eat was buttermilk and corn bread. He poured cold buttermilk over hot corn bread and mixed it together.

I learned to like it, too.

My mother was a good cook. She cooked tuna patties and white rice for breakfast (my favorite) and sometimes served that for dinner, combining it with sweet peas. We ate a lot of chicken, usually baked, but sometimes fried. And greens. My mother mixed mustard greens, turnip greens, and spinach and cooked them with smoked turkey. With a piece of corn bread on the side, we didn't go hungry. We ate a lot of pinto beans and rice, too. My mother's cheeseburgers and homemade french fries were a treat.

It was hard to be alone in an apartment full of seven people. I always had company in the bathroom. The minute I closed the door, someone yelled, "I need to use the bathroom!" If I was on the toilet, somebody was standing at the sink beside me. If I was in the bathtub, somebody sat on the toilet. Inevitably one of my sisters needed to come in if only to stand at the mirror and comb their hair.

To me, everything about life in the projects was awful. My mother was philosophical about it.

"What can you do?" she would say. "Could be worse."

The only time I could leave the apartment was to go to school. It wasn't because the neighborhood was unsafe, although it could be. The hallways were narrow and dark, and people stood around in them or sat on the stairs. Gangs sold drugs out of the buildings. At night we heard gunfire. A bullet might find you anywhere, even on the upper floors. A girl across the street was shot in the leg while lying in her bed. She lived on the tenth floor.

The reason I couldn't go outside was that I was only allowed to play with children who were Jehovah's Witnesses. I could never hang out with the people who were interesting to me. So, I stayed in the house a lot, escaped into books, and stared out the window.

My mother viewed my relationships with other kids as "bad associations." But it certainly didn't *feel* like she was protecting me from
anything. The people who were tormenting me also slept next to
me or made my meals or sat in the tub while I was on the toilet.
They were not on the playground. They were in my home.

THE FIRST TIME

One day I was playing with my brother Kirk. At least I thought we were playing. Kirk chased me around the apartment and kept rubbing my behind whenever he caught up with me. We ran in a circle around my mother while she walked down the short hallway leading from the living room to the bedrooms. At one point, I walked in front of my mother; my brother was behind her. He reached around her and started slowly rubbing my behind. I looked back at him and saw a weird grin on his face, like a joke was being played on our mother and I was in on it. I stared at him, and a numb feeling washed over me. I knew what he was doing was wrong, but I was unable to protest. I felt frozen. I never opened my mouth, didn't say anything to either him or my mom, and I couldn't believe he had done it in front of her. Our mother seemed oblivious to what was happening inches away from her. I went into my bedroom, grabbed a book, and acted like nothing had happened.

Another day, I was standing in Townsell and Kirk's room, playing with a bolo bat, bouncing the rubber ball attached to the paddle by an elastic string. Kirk came in and stood in front of me, rubbing his crotch. I stopped paddling and looked at what he was rubbing. There was something long there, underneath the material of his pants. "What's that?" I asked, pointing to the bulge as long as his zipper, going toward his leg. "The same thing that is," Kirk said, pointing toward my vagina. That didn't make sense to me. I didn't have anything like that.

"You can touch it," he said.

I shook my head no.

SHAME

In August 1975, my mother left me at home with Townsell and Kirk. We were out of school on summer break, and she went out to knock on doors and warn people about Armageddon. I was thankful she didn't drag me with her. She was a full-time "pioneer" for the Jehovah's Witnesses, which meant she spent seventy to ninety hours each month in field service, spreading the word and selling *Watchtower* and *Awake!* magazines. During the times she made me go with her, I'd walk beside her. When we saw someone walking toward us, she'd say, "Offer them a magazine." I'd hold the magazines up, trying to get their attention. Most times people looked away, but occasionally, someone would stop and talk. I hated field service. I didn't like talking to strangers, and I was deeply embarrassed when one of the kids at school saw me. They would tease me mercilessly about it the next day.

My ninth birthday was a few days away, and I wanted to stay at home and play. My oldest brother, Townsell, ignored me. He was watching back-to-back episodes of *Happy Days* on the black-and-white television on the kitchen table. Kirk, who was thirteen, started chasing me around the living room and touching my behind or rubbing my crotch when he caught me. We had never played this game before. I told myself we were playing tag. Part of me believed that. And part of me enjoyed it. It felt good to be rubbed between my legs. After about ten minutes of pretending to play tag with me he stopped, sat on the couch, and started watching TV with Townsell. I headed to the girls' bedroom. For what, I don't know. Children don't have much to do in a small apartment other than walk from room to room to see if anything has changed since the last time they were in there. They open the refrigerator door repeatedly to see if there's anything new.

As I headed to the bedroom, I looked back at my brother sitting on the couch. He turned his head and looked at me, and our eyes locked. I walked into the bedroom, picked up a book, and sat on my rollaway bed with my back against the wall. To my left was the bedroom door. Kirk came in and sat down on the bed on my right side like he wanted to read with me. Without saying a word, he reached over with his right hand and started squeezing my left breast. I kept reading like absolutely nothing was happening to me. I didn't protest. I couldn't speak.

After a few minutes, I put the book down, stood up, and walked to the other side of the room. I didn't want his hand on my breast anymore, but there was nowhere for me to go. He got up, stood beside me, and suggested that we play bunny hop. "What's a bunny hop?" I asked. "You hop around like a bunny, and I'll hop around behind you." I'd never heard of the game and had never seen anyone play it, but I was bored, and it sounded like something to do. He stood behind me with his arms around my waist.

I started hopping around the room. He held on to me from behind, humping me all the while. Bunny hopping felt like fun for a few minutes. I was leading the way. He rode my butt like a rider on a horse. I hopped to the bedroom window, stopped, and looked out. I didn't want to play that game anymore. Then I turned toward him and said, "Let's hop from the front." He looked at me with surprise and said, "Okay." I turned and faced him. He started hopping backward and pulling me toward him. I was hopping forward and trying to stay an arm's length away from him. I still thought that bunny hop could be a fun game to play. Hopping forward, I could keep him off my behind.

Kirk hopped backward from the window to the bed. Then he laid across the bed on his back, with his feet on the floor. He put both hands on my behind and pulled me down on top of him. "Not

too hard," he said, as if I was an active and willing participant. I laid
my lower body on top of his, toes on the floor, arms straight, brac-
ing myself and keeping my upper body off his. My fingers clutched
the mattress on either side of his head. I could see my brother's
terrible acne. Looking up, I stared at the bedroom door, watching
for my older brother's shadow on the hallway wall. I didn't want
him to see me.

Lying on top of my brother, genitals to genitals, clothes on, I
started to move my pelvis in a circle really fast. When he pulled my
upper body down on top of him, I stayed there, moving around,
rather than jumping off. I could have just stood up and walked out
of the room, but I didn't.

I could feel something long and straight getting harder under my
right thigh. I wondered, *Ooh, what is that?* I thought I was about to
have the sort of climax I'd been having masturbating compulsively
since I was three. But this one felt different. Suddenly something
moved and curled up right under what my mother called my
you-know-what. It balled up like a hard knot and jerked to one side.
I jumped up off my brother and backed away from the bed.

I stood there, my body turned toward the bedroom door.
Instinctively I hung my head, closed my eyes, and covered them
with my hand, deeply ashamed. I felt nasty. I had been caught
wiggling before, which made me feel embarrassed and in fear of a
whipping. I had felt like I had done something wrong, but not like
something was wrong with me. But now I felt shame. For a minute,
the experience felt good, and I had done nothing to stop it. Surely
something was terribly wrong with me. I was a bad person. I
opened my eyes and looked at my brother through my fingers. He
was still lying on his back, his hands now inside his waistband. He
was touching himself, eyes half closed, mouth hanging open. I
stood there, frozen, unable to speak. I stared at him from underneath my hand. I was waiting for him to do something. I didn't
know what was supposed to happen next.

After a minute or so, he got up and walked out of the room. He never looked at me. Like I wasn't even there. I felt used. I thought, *Aw, he ain't even gone say nuthin'!* I don't know what I wanted him to say. I think I wanted him to tell me that I wasn't a bad person. I wanted him to comfort me, tell me that everything was okay. Maybe tell me that it wasn't my fault. Maybe even tell me that he was sorry. Instead, he walked into the hallway, turned left, walked a few steps into the boys' bedroom, and closed the door. I felt humiliated. I walked out of the girls' bedroom, turned right, walked a few steps into the bathroom, and closed the door. I squeezed into the small space between the toilet and the wall, sank to the floor, and prayed to Jehovah. I asked Jehovah to forgive me for what I had done. I told Jehovah that I was sorry, that I would never do it again.

Then I got up and peed. I didn't look at myself in the bathroom mirror over the sink as I washed my hands afterward. I opened the bathroom door and went out into the living room. Townsell was still watching TV. He didn't look at me when I sat on the other end of the couch. I sat there like nothing had happened and watched *Happy Days.*

A few minutes later, our mother came home. She walked in the door and asked, "Whatchall been doing?" "Nuthin," I said. She said, "Okay." She carried her field service bag, a big purse with lots of pockets for the latest *Watchtower* and *Awake!* magazines, and the *New World Translation of the Holy Scriptures.* She put her bag on the kitchen counter and walked into the adults' bedroom. I got up from the couch and stood at the window, staring at nothing.

About an hour later, my brother came out of the boys' bedroom, said he had just woken up. "Hi, Mama," he said as he went into the kitchen, opened the refrigerator, and made a baloney and cheese sandwich. He cut it in half, sat down at the kitchen table, and stared straight ahead while he ate.

Kirk attacked me daily after that. He groped and grabbed me throughout the day, whenever I was within his reach. When I stood behind him, he would sneakily reach back and rub his fingers on my vagina. This would happen even if our parents or our siblings were just inches away. If I shampooed my hair in the kitchen sink, he would stand behind me and grind on me and fondle me while soap stung my eyes. I kicked at him and told him to stop. If I passed him in the hallway, he would dig in my vagina through my clothes from the front, and when I reached down to smack his hands away, he would quickly reach up and squeeze one of my breasts. I would instantly reach up to push his hand off my breast. He would immediately move his hand, evading mine, and, as he passed me, he would dig in my vagina through my clothes from the back. In less than twenty seconds, he would molest every private part of me. Laughing, he would then walk into the living room.

"Hi, Ma!" he would cheerfully say as if he had not done anything.

"Hi, Kirk," she would pleasantly respond.

Sometimes, after an assault, I heard loud cracking or tinkling sounds, like glass breaking inside my head.

My parents offered no help. When I yelled "Stop!" they responded with annoyance and told me to be quiet — like I was making too much noise or getting on their nerves. No one ever asked, "What's wrong?" No one ever asked, "Kirk, what are you doing?"

I dreaded being alone with Kirk. I felt used, ashamed, humiliated, and filthy. Worse, I felt like I was to blame because in the first encounter I had climbed on top of my brother when I could have jumped off. I had stayed there and wiggled because it felt good. I only stopped when it felt strange to have a climax on top of something that was moving. I denied myself the climax because it felt different from the mattress I was used to climaxing on, which of course didn't move. But up to that point, hadn't I been an active participant? Wasn't I on top of him, rubbing my you-know-what against his? "Not too hard," he had said.

I was bad. Something was wrong with me.

I had my first period right after I turned nine years old. I couldn't sleep. I felt like someone was using a jackhammer on my forehead. My migraines included light shows that rivaled the best Fourth of July fireworks. I couldn't stand to be in a room with the lights on. I vomited violently and itched continuously. The migraines sometimes came after one of my brother's daily sexual assaults. I would also have them the day before I got my period. I tried to sleep them off, but Kirk molested me in my sleep. He would stand over the bed, reaching under my clothes, digging in my vagina or my behind. Sometimes he discovered I was on my period. "Ugh," he'd say.

My body broke out in rashes. I had eczema. It first appeared on the inside of my elbows and itched like crazy. Later it showed up behind my knees and on my hands and neck. Eventually it covered my face and body. By the time I turned ten, it was so bad my mother took me to a doctor who took one look at me and handed my mother a prescription for prednisone. He did not explain the drug to my mother, or tell us about any of the potential side effects.

It hurt to bathe because water burned my skin — and forget the soap. I cried in the bathtub because of the pain. So, I stopped taking baths. My siblings called me nasty. My mother laughed when they called me names, but she never asked why I no longer bathed. When she talked to my siblings, even when I was in the room, she'd say with contempt, "I don't know *what's* wrong with her."

MAMA AND DADDY

Neither of my parents grew up in the Windy City. My father, as mentioned earlier, was from Jackson, Tennessee, and talked about it a lot. My mother was from Louisville, Mississippi, but she didn't talk about Mississippi much. She came north during the Great Migration. For many southern Blacks, Chicago was the "Promised Land" — a big city with good jobs, running water, and less racism. It wasn't, of course, but in the decades before World War II, Chicago's Black population more than doubled.

Daddy fled the South. When he was melancholy — or drunk — he talked about his family and growing up in Tennessee. When he was little, he said, he was best friends with a white boy in the neighborhood. The white boy came from a poor family and spent a lot of time with my daddy and his family. He ate dinner at my daddy's house, bathed there, and slept in the same bed as my daddy. As my father used to say, they grew up peeing all over each other.

They stayed friends as they grew up. Then my father joined the air force and went to college for a while. When he came back, he looked up his old friend. He walked up to him and started talking, happy to see him. But things had changed. His friend had become a cop — and a white man in the South. Word soon got out that my father had talked disrespectfully to a white police officer. Something bad might happen to my father, people warned. My father's parents told him to leave home. That's how he wound up living in Chicago, and he never went back to Tennessee.

I always had the feeling that, deep down, he resented his parents for pushing him out instead of standing up for him. They just said he needed to go. I don't think he ever really got over what happened. He didn't particularly care for white people after that, either.

He met my mother in Chicago. He was on the street talking to some friends when my mother walked by. "I'm going to marry that woman," he said. "Excuse me," he added, interrupting his friends, "I need to tell her." He followed her to the grocery store, and they were together ever since.

My mother was five foot seven, the color of milk chocolate, and — when I was growing up — about sixty pounds overweight. She had a round face, a small gap between her two front teeth, and thin, short hair, but that didn't matter because she never left home without wearing one of her long-haired wigs, makeup, and dark-red lipstick. "You can't always control how you feel, but you can always control how you look," she said.

My father was a handsome man. He was just shy of six feet, mocha brown, with broad, square shoulders and a round belly that looked like he'd swallowed a basketball. He had a ready smile and kind eyes. His black hair was silky and curly. He preferred to keep it cut close around the sides and longer at the top.

I don't think they were happy. There were times — fleeting moments — when they laughed together, but they spent a lot of time ignoring each other. And when they spoke, they often argued. They yelled and shouted. "You think everybody's crazy except you!" my father would say. "You're drunk all the time!" my mother would respond. "If you feel like you need another man, go get you one," my father yelled. To which my mother would say, "I will." My father would immediately get remorseful — almost tearful — and say, "Honey, please don't leave me." And she wouldn't. My father swore all the time when he was drunk. He cursed when he was sober, too, if he was losing an argument with my mother — which was often since she never admitted fault. Then he would cover his mouth and say, "Oops!" like it was an accident. He would say to my mother, "Now see what you made me do!"

My father was not particularly religious in the beginning. He loved politics and watched the news daily. He watched baseball games on TV and rooted for the Cubs. And he loved to read. My mother *taught* me how to read, but my *love* of reading came from my father. He read Black-themed fiction from the 1970s, the *Chicago Sun-Times*, and nasty magazines like *Hustler* and *Playboy*, which he hid in a sock drawer.

My father loved to laugh and tell jokes. He listened to jazz and the blues, and he sang in a high, trembling voice. "Good Night, Irene" was a favorite song. But he didn't listen to music in the house much. My mother played cassette tapes featuring music from the Jehovah's Witness songbook, mostly slow hymns based on Scripture. The words to the songs came from the *New World Translation of the Holy Scriptures*, the Jehovah's Witness Bible. Sometimes Daddy would play his vinyl records when my mother wasn't home. He would walk around the apartment, singing and smiling. But when my mother came home, he turned the record player off.

Daddy had been in the air force, but he never received military benefits. The air force gave him an administrative discharge. He said it was because he didn't get along with his commanding officer. It wasn't a dishonorable discharge, but it wasn't an honorable discharge, either. Basically, the air force kicked him out.

He was a frustrated man. He was passive and craved approval. He resented my mother's controlling personality but depended on her caretaking. Early on, he worked as a laborer and a security guard. Before we moved to the projects, he came home from work each day, but he always hated menial jobs because his IQ was higher than 140. "That's genius level," he said.

After we moved to the projects, he changed. He didn't work, and I never knew why. I never asked, either. He spent his days drinking, usually in the empty lot across the street. He would drink with the other neighborhood drunks until dark, then stagger home. He yelled and screamed a lot. My mother didn't stop him. Eventually, my mother convinced him to join her religious group. After that, when he tried to discuss politics, my mother stopped him. She dismissed all talk about aldermen, mayors, and even presidents. "Nothing matters except Jehovah's Kingdom," she said.

SISTERS AND BROTHERS

When my mother met my father, she already had two children: my sister Annette, or Net, born in 1953, and my sister Cheryl, born in 1958. After meeting my father in late 1960, my mother quickly had three more children: Townsell in 1961, Kirk in 1962, and Faye in 1963. But they didn't marry until 1966. I was born a few months after that. My mother kept our baby pictures and family photos under a glass top that covered the coffee table in the dining room. One day my father and a couple of his friends were drinking wine in the living room. One of them spilled his glass. The wine seeped under the tabletop and destroyed every picture.

I don't know a lot about my sister Net. She once told me, "Girl, I can tell you some stories that will curl your hair." But when I asked her to tell me, she said, "I can't because I don't know who you talk to." It's a strange family. I know Net had a difficult childhood, but I wasn't around for most of it, since she he was thirteen years my senior. One of her daughters died shortly after birth. She had a hole in her heart.

Net and our mother fought a lot when Net was a teenager. Once they even came to blows, my father said. Net ran away from home a lot, and she spent time in a home for juvenile delinquents when I was just a baby. Physically, we're very much alike. We're the same height, five foot six inches, with the same dark-brown complexion. We're also the only siblings who always wore glasses. She moved into the projects with us after the breakup of her third marriage.

My sister Cheryl constantly spied on me. If I did something wrong, she squealed on me. One day I closed the bedroom door and danced to a song on the radio. Jehovah's Witnesses forbade "worldly" dancing. Only square dancing was allowed. I heard a noise at the door and jerked it open. Cheryl squatted on the other side, watching me through the keyhole.

"Ma, come see what Lisa doing!" she exclaimed.

"Whatchu doing?" my mother asked.

Cheryl stood beside her and grinned triumphantly.

Cheryl was Mama's favorite. Eight years older than me, she looked like a younger version of Mama, right down to the small gap between her two front teeth. She learned early that the way to Mama's heart was to pour herself into a mold of Mama's making.

Cheryl could have stopped the others from mistreating me. Instead, she joined in the torment. In fact, she often initiated it. One day, when I was eleven and Cheryl was nineteen, I sat on my bed reading a book. For a rare moment, I was alone, unbothered. Cheryl came into the bedroom. "Lisa, come into the kitchen for a minute." "What for?" I asked. "Just come here." Reluctantly, I put my book down and joined Cheryl and Faye in the kitchen. Cheryl pointed to two glasses of red Kool-Aid on the kitchen counter. "Pick one," she said.

I stared at Cheryl. I hadn't asked for any Kool-Aid. Then I looked at the glasses. One glass was one-third full. The other was half full. "Make them both the same," I said. "Just pick one," Cheryl responded, standing back from the glasses, watching me. I didn't understand why there wasn't an equal amount of Kool-Aid in both glasses. Since Faye was also standing there, I assumed the other drink was for her. I wanted her to have the same amount.

"Why don't you make them the same?" I pleaded.

"Just pick one," Cheryl repeated while Faye stood and watched.

Confused, I grabbed the largest drink and walked back to my room with my head down. I felt bad because I thought I was greedy to pick the glass with the most Kool-Aid. Then I heard Cheryl fill the remaining glass to the brim while she and Faye laughed hysterically.

Of all Mama's children, Cheryl was the only one who claimed complete devotion to the Jehovah's Witnesses. As a result, in our house, Cheryl could do no wrong. And she knew it.

Faye was the baby of the family, at least until I came along three years later. She constantly competed with me for our mother's attention. She characterized all my actions as "wrong," then tried to get Mama to agree with her. Faye was a couple of inches taller than me, with size ten feet. When we were growing up, she would wear my size eight shoes, which I bought with money I earned from part-time jobs. She would never ask. When I would protest, our mother would take her side. "You shouldn't mind!" she would scream at me. Our mother, and Cheryl, also wore size ten shoes. Faye's big feet stretched my shoes so much that after she wore them I had to stuff them with toilet paper to keep them from flopping off my feet.

Whenever we ate chicken, my mother would split the breast between my father and Faye. I wanted the breast, too. I never argued about my father getting the piece of the chicken he preferred, but why did my sister always get the breast? Why couldn't I get it sometimes? "Your sister won't eat anything else," my mother said. "But you will."

My sister wouldn't eat anything else because she knew she didn't have to. I learned two life lessons at the dinner table, lessons that stuck with me for many years. One, I could never get what I wanted. Two, other people were more important than me. If I wanted something, and someone else wanted the same thing, they would get it. Mama hammered home that message every time she cooked chicken — which was all the time.

At home, Mama coddled her sons. They had no chores or responsibilities — and no discipline.

My oldest brother, Townsell, is named after our father, but one of my aunts said my mother was pregnant with Townsell *before* she met my father. Townsell started drinking in his early teens. He didn't drink at home, but he would come home tipsy. Rather than punish him, my mother would make excuses for his drinking. One day she told my father, "It's *your* fault that he drinks!" Townsell had his problems, and I had mine. He didn't pick on me as much as my other siblings did, but he didn't defend me, either. As a result, I couldn't stand him any more than I could stand any of the others.

Although he was baptized as a Jehovah's Witness, he was disfellowshipped in his late teens "for conduct unbecoming a Christian." I'm not sure if it was for drinking, fornication, or both. Even though he was no longer a Jehovah's Witness, Mama gave him money for booze and drugs until his early forties. She met him in deserted parking lots and slipped him cash out of the driver's window. It looked like a drug deal. Mama thought my father didn't know what she was doing, but he did. "She's always giving my money to Townsell," he complained one day after she left home.

Unlike Townsell, Kirk was never baptized as a Jehovah's Witness. I don't know why not. My mother made us all go to the Kingdom Hall together. Maybe Kirk couldn't bring himself to get baptized while he knew he was sexually molesting me.

Because I was only eight years old when Kirk started abusing me, I don't have a lot of memories of him that don't involve him attacking me. I do remember that he was a good swimmer. He even competed on the high school swim team. He also taught himself to ride a bicycle. Sometimes the family watched him from the window. He practiced right after daybreak on Saturday and Sunday mornings in the parking lot across the street. Eventually, he became a good rider.

"You said you were going to do it, and you did it!" my mother said, beaming.

What can I say about my brother?

I could feel his hands on me even when he wasn't there.

I NEED A KNIFE

I loved pennies. Whenever anyone gave me any money — I sometimes ran errands for people at the Kingdom Hall — I always
converted the bills to pennies. Usually, the man who owned the
nearby candy store would give me pennies as change. Shiny, dull,
bent, scarred: I kept them in jars under my bed. I loved having
money. I would carefully count my pennies and keep a record of
how much money I had. I lovingly dusted off the jars.

One day when I was eleven, Faye and my mother were huddled
in front of the living room window, whispering. Suddenly my
mother turned to me and said, "Lisa, I need to use your pennies."
Faye needed bus fare.

I opened my mouth to protest, but my mother interrupted me
before I could make a sound.

"Girl, GIVE me those pennies, I NEED them!" my mother
shouted.

I felt like I was being robbed. Why didn't my sister ask me for the
money? Why did she ask our mother to take it from me? And why
did Mama agree?

I placed my penny jars on the kitchen table. Mama emptied
them and gave the money to my sister, who had never saved
anything. Faye laughed as she gathered up my pennies and left the
house. I don't know what happened to the money — she clearly
didn't need all of it for the bus.

I stopped putting pennies in jars after that. Instead, I spent
everything I got. I thought, *It's pointless for me to save it if someone
is just going to take it.*

Everyone robbed me. It started early. In kindergarten, I had a pink toy watch that I wore to school. One day, the teacher let me go to the bathroom, and a tall, older girl was already in there.

"Gimme that watch," she said.

I stared at her and froze. Then I took off the watch and handed it to her. I was too numb to protest. And she was much bigger than me. She snatched it and walked out of the bathroom. I used the toilet and went back to class. I acted like nothing had happened. The girl wasn't in my class, and I didn't know who she was. I never told the teacher what happened. But when we got out of school, my sisters and brothers were waiting for me so that we could walk home together. I told them what had happened, and they ran around looking for the girl, but we couldn't find her. I couldn't even remember what she looked like. I never got my watch back.

In high school, I entered a contest and won a radio cassette player. It was just a radio cassette player, but it was *my* radio cassette player. I had something of my own. I walked around with it and made tapes of my favorite songs off the radio — songs like "Endless Love" by Diana Ross and Lionel Richie, "Being with You" by Smokey Robinson, and "How 'Bout Us" by Champaign.

I even slept with it, listening to the music with headphones. Eventually, I asked my mother if I could put the player in her bedroom closet for safekeeping. I knew that if I left it in the room I shared with my sisters, they would use it without my permission. My mother agreed to keep it. One day I looked for it in her closet. It wasn't there. She had given it to my brother Townsell, and I never saw it again.

This was my life. If I turned on a light to read, somebody turned it off. If I tried to sleep in a darkened room, somebody turned on a light. If I opened a door, somebody closed it. If I watched TV, somebody would change the channel. If I fled to another room, somebody else would need that room, too. If I left my chair for a minute, somebody took it. If I had to go to the bathroom, somebody joined me.

One time I cleaned the bathtub and ran some bathwater. Before I could get into the tub, Townsell knocked on the door. I dressed and stepped out so that he could use the toilet. He saw the tub full of water and took a bath. I stood outside the door, screaming. "Townsell, get out of my water!"

He finished bathing and came out wearing a towel. He walked by me like I wasn't there. I went into the bathroom. The tub was filthy. I cried and pleaded, "Ma, make Townsell wash out the tub!" My mother stood in the kitchen, along with Cheryl. They laughed hysterically. Instead of filling the dirty tub with water, I crouched over the drain and washed myself as the water ran. Cheryl opened the door and came in. She stood in the bathroom, looked at me, and said, "Ma, Lisa in here taking a bath in a dirty tub!"

My mother marched into the bathroom and looked at me with disgust.

"How could you?" she roared, a look of shock and loathing on her face.

She and Cheryl shook their heads and left.

"Ugh," Cheryl said as she closed the door behind them.

My siblings could do no wrong, and I could do no right. Nobody cared what happened to me. My brother molested me, my sisters bullied me constantly, my father hid in the bedroom watching TV, and my mother thought everything that befell me was funny.

Meanwhile, Armageddon could start at any moment.

Not only did I feel like a bad person, I also felt hopeless. Each time I told Kirk to stop, he ignored me. Sometimes I would freeze — a kind of shock. But it was more than that. The human body is designed to respond favorably to sexual arousal. It is a normal physiological response to feel good when someone touches you. So, there were times when I would stand there long enough to feel pleasure. On those occasions, I felt like a nasty person who deserved what was happening to me.

The weight of a secret of this magnitude made me feel crazy. I was just a little girl. I wanted to run and play and have friends. But I couldn't do any of that. I didn't feel like playing. I was depressed. I retreated into books and created elaborate mental fantasies about being rescued and taken away. In my mind, I replayed the things that had been done to me — a symptom of post-traumatic stress disorder.

I felt under constant threat, like anybody could do anything to me at any time, and I would be powerless to stop them.

I felt like I needed a knife.

MOUNT OLYMPUS

My school life was anything but typical. I learned to read at three and began kindergarten at four. My teachers then recommended that I skip the first and seventh grades. I had no say in the matter. School officials told my parents I was bored with my classes and was reading well above grade level. My parents thought it was a good idea. In a rare move, my mother praised my intelligence after speaking with my teachers.

"Lisa, you're smart," she said.

After school, I'd walk home by myself, and whenever my sisters or I came through the door from school, we'd ask the same thing: "Daddy hollering?" In other words: *Is he drunk?* If the answer was yes, we'd slip into our rooms before he could curse at us or slap us on the head.

My mother, meanwhile, did her best to protect us from an immoral world. She worried we would become "demonized" by reading the wrong books or watching bad TV shows or listening to sensual pop songs. Unfortunately, she saw sex, immorality, and demons in everything. I listened to the Jackson 5 and Donnie and Marie Osmond, but my mother fretted daily about the collapse of the world's nations, including the US. The Bible prophesied, "Sudden destruction is to be instantly on them . . . and they will by no means escape."

On top of that, she scrambled to raise six children while living with an alcoholic husband and paying the bills with a welfare check. The fight for women's rights, the environmental movement, Watergate, the energy crisis, riots, racial tension, *Star Wars*, *Star Trek*, disco, the Black Panther Party — they weren't a part of her world, so they weren't a part of ours, either. We lived in an anxious, airtight bubble of my mother's fears.

She monitored everything that came into the house. We couldn't watch *Bewitched* or *I Dream of Jeannie* — shows that featured magic. Instead, we viewed *Gilligan's Island*, *Happy Days*, *The Partridge Family*, *The Brady Bunch*, and *Good Times* — shows with well-adjusted families, even if *The Flintstones* lived in the Stone Age.

The search for the good life — *Happy Days*, indeed — was a frequent theme in the religious magazines we handed to strangers. One cover showed a smiling father hoisting a little girl into the air. "A Secure Future: How You Can Find It," the headline read. Another illustration showed a father greeting his son, his arms stretched wide. People everywhere desire security, the author said. "Is such security possible?"

I skipped first grade and seventh grade, which meant that my classmates were always older than me. They didn't want to hang out with me, and not being Jehovah's Witnesses, my mother wouldn't allow me to be friends with them anyway.

You would think that, with all the sisters and brothers I had, I would have had plenty of people to play with. But I was the loneliest child in the world.

I turned to books for company.

Sometimes the only thing that kept me from killing myself was the thought, *Maybe something good will happen today.* Often that good thing was a kindness from a teacher.

One of my eighth-grade teachers, Miss Sadie Wilson, threw me a lifeline. She knew I was bored with school. "Maybe you could help me grade papers," she said. I understood the material, and she trusted me to get it right.

Once she realized I could read well above my grade level, she loaned me books from her home library. They weren't the kinds of books the Jehovah's Witnesses would approve, but my mother allowed me to read books assigned as homework. Beyond that, I could only read *Watchtower* and *Awake!*. In fact, I *had* to read them. My mother conducted weekly Bible studies at home, and we sat around the kitchen table and answered questions based on our reading. *Watchtower* focused on surviving Armageddon and joining Jehovah. *Awake!* featured more interesting articles about current events, everything from obesity to the collapse of the American family. Of course, the authors interpreted those events through a religious lens. It's not like we were reading the *Chicago Tribune*.

Miss Wilson widened my world. She loaned me books about Greek and Roman mythology, a topic she particularly enjoyed. She always asked me if I liked reading about the different gods. When I said yes, she became excited. She had no children; I assumed I was the daughter she never had. Since the books came from a teacher, my mother okayed them. They had intriguing titles like *Timeless Tales of Gods and Heroes* and *The Complete World of Greek Mythology*. In my room I read about Odysseus, King Midas, and the Amazons — strong, independent women who had rebelled against a male-dominated society. On Mount Olympus, a peak that touched the clouds, the gods dined on ambrosia and nectar.

One of my favorite stories was about Athena, the Greek goddess of intelligence and wisdom, courage, law and justice, warfare, and mathematics. No mother gave birth to Athena. She sprang from her father Zeus's head, fully grown, wearing a full set of armor, ready to defend herself.

Athena was everything I wished I could be.

The gods and goddesses of the ancient world interested me far more than the drab material I was allowed to read at home, books and magazines published by the Watchtower Bible and Tract Society. But none of my peers were interested in mythology, which made me feel even more like an outsider.

I had always been a child who asked a lot of questions. Rarely did the people in my orbit have the answers. I wanted to know why Jehovah's Witnesses thought Jesus was the only person who had a god for a father. I was reading lots of stories about people who were part human and part god, Greeks who were the gods of earthquakes, the sea, the heavens. Could Jesus be a myth? I asked. Who wrote the Bible — the same people who wrote the myths? At times, the stories in the Bible were like those in the Greek and Roman mythology books. The adults I knew tried to answer me, but their responses usually made no sense. The religious people I knew bristled at my questioning the Bible. It made me feel like no one understood me.

Because I had skipped two grades, I was too young chronologically to be with the older kids in my grade, and I was too old mentally to be with kids my age. I felt out of sync with everybody, in purgatory at school and hell at home. Jehovah's Witnesses believed that only a small number of faithful Christians — 144,000, to be exact — would go to heaven to rule with Christ in the Kingdom of God.

Where could I go? Mount Olympus?

ROMANCE

My world changed when I turned twelve: First, I started high school. I had graduated from eighth grade in June, when I was eleven, and I turned twelve in August.

Second, my brother Kirk moved in with Net, our oldest sister. After four years, he would no longer molest me every day at home. But he still groped and fondled me whenever he had a reason to come around. And anyway, the damage had been done. I remained depressed and suicidal — not that anyone appeared to notice or care.

In this state of mind, I started my first day at Martin Luther King High School on South Drexel Boulevard, a few blocks from the projects. For weeks I had begged my mother to send me to the Paul Laurence Dunbar Vocational High School instead. But my other siblings had all gone to King High School. One of my sisters scoffed at my request.

"Who do you think you are?" she asked.

My mother laughed. "Dunbar is too far away," she said. "You would need bus fare every day. Besides," she said, "the *name* of the school doesn't matter. Only the effort you put into your studies."

I wasn't alone in my assessment of King High School. Before I left the eighth grade, my homeroom teacher quizzed the class about their futures. "What high school did you pick?" he asked. He sat at his desk, called each student's name, and wrote down their answers. When he called my name and I said, "King," his head jerked up. He looked at me, startled. The other kids in the class laughed. He looked down at his paper, shook his head sadly, and wrote "King" next to my name.

Shortly after I enrolled in King, a staff member called me down to the administration office. She wanted to verify my age. She assumed someone had gotten it wrong. "How old are you?" she asked. "Twelve," I said. She stared at me with astonishment and then said loudly, "If *my* child was only twelve and in high school, I would *shole* have them in a better school than *this!*"

I hung my head and went back to class, wishing she was my mother.

Life at King was a nightmare. I sat in ninth-grade classes with a bunch of fourteen- and fifteen-year-olds, some of whom couldn't read. The older students called me a "JEE-hovah Witness." Once again, no one befriended me or talked to me during lunch. My head hurt and my stomach burned all the time. I *should* have been transferred to a better school, maybe even a place for gifted children. Most parents would want that for their children. But my mother was too busy waiting for the world to end.

In the tenth grade, I looked forward to taking a class in algebra. But the class, taught by a Holocaust survivor, was a disaster. Every day the bell rang, we sat down, and the teacher wrote some numbers on the board. A few minutes later, someone in the back would yell, "Heil Hitler!" and the teacher would start screaming, red in the face. The students in the back would run out of the room with the teacher in hot pursuit. For forty-five minutes, I would sit in a noisy class with no teacher and read. The same thing would happen pretty much every day, or at least that's how I remember it.

The experience didn't quash my interest in numbers. Math relied on order and logic — the exact opposite of my home life, where fear, chaos, and judgment ruled. Answers to math problems never displeased God. Wrong answers didn't make me a disobedient person. How could I not love algebra? The word originated from the Arabic word *al-Jabr*, meaning "the reunion of broken parts."

It was a far cry from home, where if I questioned something, I was told, "This is what the *elders* say. Now, who do you think *you* are?"

Miserable, I found ways to escape my school and home life. My older sister Net read Harlequin romance novels, and after she moved out I started reading them, too. I got a part-time job in the high school office and bought more novels at a nearby drugstore. The piles of books in my bedroom comforted me. And the stories featured everything missing from my life: exotic places, handsome men, beautiful women, love. I also started reading teen magazines about beauty, skin care, and hairstyles.

My other escape, which was just as important, was to spend spring break and summers with my aunts and uncles in Milwaukee, especially Aunt Amie, the youngest of my mother's siblings. She stood about five foot eight, an inch or so taller than my mother. She went to the Kingdom Hall for a while but eventually decided it wasn't for her. She worked nights as a data processor at a local hospital while her husband, Junior, worked during the day at a factory. When I stayed with them, one of them was always at home, and it made me feel like I had a parent.

Aunt Amie always greeted me warmly, which contrasted with the coldness I'd grown to expect from my mother. I also liked the fact that they didn't live in the projects. We did things I never did at home, like go out for ice cream on a warm summer evening. Sometimes after dinner we would walk around the neighborhood. It felt like a different world to me.

My aunt Irene, my mother's other sister, and her husband, Uncle Henry, and their son also lived in a nice house in Milwaukee. Aunt Irene worked at Miller Beer, and Uncle Henry was a Milwaukee police officer.

Whenever I stayed at either house, I had my own room. Aunt Irene and Uncle Henry had a piano and a Ping-Pong table in the basement. I could go outside in the yard. When I stayed with either of my aunts, I felt like I could breathe.

My mother ruined one of my last school breaks. When I returned from Aunt Amie's house, I discovered that my mother had thrown all my romance novels into a dumpster.

"Why did you do that?" I asked.

"You didn't need to be reading that," she said.

SHUNNED

One day I angered my mother when I asked her for something. She was cooking spaghetti. My sister Cheryl stood in the kitchen with her.

My mother said to me, "I'm sick of you. The better I treat you, the worse you act. As far as I'm concerned, you can just go kill yourself. I don't even care."

Cheryl walked over, looked me in the face, and laughed. I stood there for a minute, in silence, stunned. Since I had just been thinking about jumping out of the window, I wondered if she had read my mind. Maybe I really should just jump.

I walked into my bedroom and closed the door. I picked up a book and started reading.

A few minutes later, my mother opened the door.

"What you doing?" she asked.

"Reading," I said.

"I can see that, Lisa. What you reading?"

"A book."

"What's the *name* of the book?"

I looked at the cover and read the title.

She looked at me like she couldn't stand me. Then she slammed the door and went away.

Jehovah's Witnesses divide the world between "the sheep" and "the goats." If you're a Jehovah's Witness, you're a sheep. Surviving Armageddon depends on your staying "in the flock." Everyone outside of the flock is a goat destined to be destroyed by Jehovah. The division comes straight from the Bible, Matthew 25:32: "He will separate people one from another, just as a shepherd separates the sheep from the goats."

Like every other teenager, I was trying to form an identity in the environment I was in. Nobody ever asked me what I wanted to be when I grew up. In fact, because I wasn't a Jehovah's Witness, I expected that I wouldn't live long enough to grow up. Jehovah was going to kill me at any moment, when Armageddon started.

One day, when I was about fourteen and in eleventh grade, I walked into the living room and announced, "I guess I'm just a goat."

My family, slumped on the couch and in chairs, had been watching a TV show. My father chuckled. Then he and my siblings stared at my mother. They were waiting for a cue from her as to how they should respond. I had proclaimed my place in Jehovah's universe.

Mother looked at me with disdain, then turned to the TV screen. "It's blurry," she said. My father got up and tinkered with the back of the set.

My mother spoke with the elders at the Kingdom Hall about me. Jehovah's Witnesses shun people who leave the organization, including their family members. Mothers and fathers disown their children. Children stop talking to their parents. Siblings stop speaking to each other. Family members refuse to eat at the same dinner table with relatives. They go to the Kingdom Hall and call one another sister so-and-so and brother so-and-so. Then they come home and refuse to speak to their biological sisters, brothers, and children.

The elders were men in their forties and fifties who wore three-piece suits and carried the Jehovah's Witness version of the Bible, the *New World Translation of the Holy Scriptures*. They met with me, told me Armageddon was near, and announced to the congregation that I was on "public reproof." A baptized member who leaves the religion is "disfellowshipped," but since I had never been baptized, "public reproof" was the severest punishment I could get. The result was the same. My mother, father, siblings, and everyone I had grown up with shunned me. If I said, "Good morning," they said nothing. I sat on my bed, lonelier than ever.

For more than a dozen years, I had been allowed to associate with other Jehovah's Witnesses. When the organization shunned me, everyone I knew stopped speaking to me. They would pass me on the street and look the other way.

I used to go to the same hair salon as one of the Jehovah's Witnesses in the Kenwood congregation. One rainy Saturday morning, I stood at the locked door of the salon and knocked. I had an appointment to style my hair. The salon doors were locked to prevent people from entering the business and robbing everyone at gunpoint — a routine occurrence in the area.

The rain splashed on my head and clothes.

"I'll get it," I heard someone say in response to my knock.

A woman approached the door to let me in out of the rain. She was a Jehovah's Witness. As she got closer, she recognized me. She came to the door, looked at me, turned, and walked away.

It started thundering.

IN THE LOOP

No one celebrated my fourteenth birthday, of course, as Jehovah's Witnesses are not allowed to acknowledge birthdays, but I did convince my mother to send me to Jones Commercial High School, which helped students get jobs. The board of education had even designed it to look like a six-story office building. The teenage girls wore dresses, hats, and gloves to class; the boys wore suits and ties. It felt very '50s. The students were a little friendlier than in my previous schools, in part because they *wanted* to be there.

I took the bus to high school. I could see the bus from our living room window when it was about five minutes away. I ran downstairs and quickly walked one block to the stop, catching the bus without having to stand outside for a long time waiting for it. Every day my sister Cheryl, in her twenties but still living at home, would wait until I announced, "Okay, I see the bus! I'm gone!" Then, as I stepped out the front door, she would call out behind me, "Lisa, what you have on doesn't look right." I would close the door behind me, her laughter mingling with my mother's as I left. One day when she did it again, I stopped at the front door, turned around, and screamed, "Cheryl, you do this every day! Every day you sit in this house and watch me while I'm getting dressed! You see me when I'm combing my hair! You see me when I'm putting on my clothes! If you think something doesn't look right, why don't you ever say anything about it until I'm about to walk out the door? Why don't you say something earlier, when I would still have time to do something about it, rather than waiting until you hear me say the bus is coming, and then tell me something is wrong — when it's too late for me to change it?"

Sitting at the kitchen table with our mother, Cheryl played the victim. "I didn't mean anything by it! It looks okay. Just go!" she said. My mother looked at me as if I had attacked Cheryl. She sat up straighter in her chair, as if she was preparing to leap to Cheryl's defense. My father was standing in the kitchen. He closed the refrigerator door and looked at my mother, slowly shaking his head. He acted as if my behavior was inexplicable to him, and he could not understand what was wrong with me. Cheryl looked back and forth between our parents, with a hurt look on her face. I walked out, closing the door behind me.

I had missed the bus.

Jones Commercial High School stood on a block in downtown Chicago next door to a homeless shelter for men. I studied court reporting and entered various statewide competitions based on speed and accuracy. I won them all.

At first, I worked part-time as an office clerk after school. As a senior, I worked at an after-school job typing, answering phones, and filing papers at Household Finance Corporation, a company in Chicago's downtown Loop.

I didn't want to be a secretary. I loved math and science; I wanted to be a chemist or a scientist. I kept a folded poster of the periodic table under my mattress, but that dream seemed far away. Jones was a commercial high school, not a college prep school. No one counseled me on how to apply to a university. My parents never discussed it, especially my mother, who saw no value in "worldly knowledge." She said the end of the world was coming, and anyone who wasn't a Jehovah's Witness would die. The world's true believers would survive and live in a paradise on earth.

Who needed higher learning in paradise?

I graduated from high school in 1982. I didn't buy a copy of the high school yearbook — why bother? The world was coming to an end. I didn't sit for a yearbook photo, and I didn't go to the prom — I couldn't date.

Instead of helping me move into a dorm room, my mother took me to the Illinois Department of Labor to get a worker's permit. We didn't own a car. We took a bus downtown, and my mother filled out a simple form stating that she approved of my entering the workforce. She got it notarized while we waited. I didn't argue with her because it was pointless to do so. I had no options. The truth was, since I wasn't going to college, I wanted to earn some money. Having a job would give me a reason to get out of the apartment. I didn't want to sit at home, and I didn't want to spend my days walking door-to-door with my mother, preaching and doling out magazines that asked, "Would you like to live in happiness and peace with true justice on earth?" Of course you would.

After graduation, some of my classmates headed off to college. I got a job as a secretary at Lloyd's of London in downtown Chicago.

I was fifteen.

JAMES

At Lloyd's of London I worked with fifteen other secretaries in their late twenties or early thirties, most of them Black. The manager, a middle-aged white woman, sat at a desk at the front of the room. The proofreader, an older white woman with gray hair, sat next to her. The secretaries grabbed insurance claims from the stacks on the manager's desk and entered the information into the company's database. The manager tracked our progress. Her desk faced mine.

I didn't like the work — it was tedious, and it was irrelevant to my sixteen-year-old life — but I enjoyed working in Chicago's bustling downtown. Successful people filled the Loop: men in suits and ties and women in skirt suits and heels. I wanted to be successful, too. But I made minimum wage; my lunch was a fish sandwich and small fries from McDonald's. Sometimes I went to the nearby Popeye's, where I ordered a spicy chicken breast with fries and coleslaw. Occasionally I ate dinner at Popeye's if the weather was nice and I dreaded going home.

Repairmen from Exxon Office Systems worked on our computers and printers. The equipment broke down all the time, so we saw a lot of repairmen.

One day my printer stopped working. A twenty-one-year-old technician named James Bankston worked on it. He was tall and handsome. We chatted while he worked at my desk. I thought he was fine. As he was leaving, he asked me if I had seen the movie *48 Hrs*.

"No, I haven't," I said with anticipation.

"I was going to go see it on Friday. Would you like to go?"

I was sixteen, but I didn't look it. He didn't ask my age.

That Friday, I left work and met James at his job. Downtown Chicago was awash in holiday decorations. Even though I had never celebrated Christmas because of the Jehovah's Witnesses' proscription against it, I had always enjoyed the holidays. It got dark early, and by 5:00 P.M., the Loop resembled a beautiful Black lady decked out in her finest jewels. Twinkling stars adorned the streetlights. Holiday decorations, each more intricate than the next, crowded shop windows. Sweets from the department store candy counters at Carson Pirie Scott and Marshall Field's, carolers singing "Joy to the World," the musical clang of ringing bells — I loved it all.

James wanted a drink, so we walked to a nearby bar before the show. I had never tasted alcohol, but I didn't tell him that. He ordered a rum and Coke. When he asked me what I would like, I said uncertainly, "White wine?" He asked the bartender to bring me a glass, and I took a couple of sips, but I didn't like it.

Shortly afterward, we walked to the theater. I pretended to enjoy the movie's action scenes more than I did because James was so into them, but Eddie Murphy's made me laugh. James sat next to the aisle, and I sat to his left. He kept his left arm around me throughout the movie, and I rested my head on his shoulder.

He also kissed me throughout the movie, but his advances made me uncomfortable, because they lacked romance.

In the Harlequin romance novels I'd been reading for several years, the man was always electrifying. The woman's heart throbbed when he was near. We did not look deeply into each other's eyes, and James never asked if he could kiss me. He just kept matter-of-factly kissing me when my lips were within reach. Just like Kirk had matter-of-factly groped and fondled me whenever my body was near, and I felt violated.

I didn't like a lot of things about James, but living with abuse had taught me to ignore my feelings. I saw James as a way out of my parents' apartment, and I believed the romance would come later.

I still wanted to see him. James might not have been a Harlequin romance hero, but he had a house, a good job, and a car. And he wanted me.

As my mother always said, "Could be worse."

We saw each other once a week. Sometimes we would go for a drive, get something to eat, and then go back to his house. James owned a duplex at 6228 South Claremont Avenue. His mother lived with him on the first floor, and his sister lived on the second floor with her teenage son. James introduced me to each of them, and they seemed friendly.

His mother was often at home when I visited. When she wasn't around, James and I would have sex either in his bedroom or on the living room sofa. During sex, I thought about being molested by my brother Kirk. It felt repulsive to think about my brother while I was with James, but I couldn't help it. Usually, I just checked out and stared at the ceiling until it was over. Then James would sit on the sofa and smoke weed. One time he tried to pass the joint to me.

"You want some?" he asked. I was seated on the sofa, to his left.

"No, that's okay."

"Oh, come on."

"No, I don't want any," I repeated, annoyed.

He inhaled deeply and, without warning, leaned across me, forcing me to lean back on the arm of the couch. He pinned my arms down. Not knowing what he was about to do, I struggled. I couldn't get my arms free.

He put his face next to mine and blew marijuana smoke up my nose. He held me down until I had to inhale.

"You're going to feel that," he said.

He unpinned my arms and sat back up. He looked over at me and laughed, and took another hit.

I sat up and stared straight ahead. I felt furious, violated, and disrespected, but also the usual sense of numbness, and of being frozen. I now know my familiar reaction was what scientists and psychologists call tonic immobility, a defensive response to trauma, but I had no awareness of this back then.

A couple of hours later, he drove me home. He knew I was upset, but he didn't care. He thought it was funny.

Three months after I started dating James, I began to feel tired and extra sleepy. I felt queasy but didn't throw up. My mother took me to the public health clinic. I hadn't told her I was having sex. She would never have taken me to the doctor so I could get on the pill. She would have just told me, "Stop committing fornication." So I'd relied on the rhythm method instead. When the doctor told me that I was pregnant, I was surprised. I thought the rhythm method was reliable.

"It's not the end of the world," she said gently.

I wasn't happy, but I wasn't unhappy, either. "I'll take care of the baby," James assured me. At last, I would have someone to love. Even better, James wasn't some teenage boy with nothing. And he wasn't some guy who sold drugs on the street corner, like a lot of other guys in the neighborhood where I lived. My home life was still awful, but I could see good things ahead of me. James owned a house, which I assumed would become our home. Having a house of my own would be a big leap from the projects, and I saw our baby growing up there. I pictured myself being a stay-at-home mom, getting up in the morning and fixing breakfast for my husband before he headed off to work.

My dreams were just that: dreams. James worked long hours, and I seldom saw him. On top of that, a doctor diagnosed his mother with cancer, and after that I rarely saw or even heard from him. He never mentioned my moving out of my parents' apartment and into his duplex with him. Miserable and rejected, I plunged into a deep depression.

May 1983 was unusually chilly; high temperatures hovered in the low fifties. Meteorologists said it was Chicago's tenth-coldest May on record. Then, in early June, temperatures jumped into the low eighties. The rest of the summer was brutally hot, with more than forty days reaching into the nineties. July included two days of one hundred degrees. Weather-wise, it was a freakish year of extremes. A few months before Mercedes was born, my mother took me down to a crowded welfare office. Oscillating fans circulated the hot air. Most of the women in the waiting area had young children or crying babies with them. Some people had to stand. After waiting all morning, I finally saw a welfare worker.

I was seven months pregnant when I turned seventeen that August. Every day I got up and wobbled down six flights of dark, urine-soaked steps, walked two blocks to the bus stop, took the bus to the El and the El to the Loop. One morning I couldn't find a seat on the train. Nobody moved. I grabbed a strap and closed my eyes. The jerking motion of the train made me throw up. Vomit splashed onto people around me. I was embarrassed and apologized to all of them, but nobody reacted angrily. If anything, they seemed to feel sorry for me.

I stopped working a couple of weeks later. The terrible eczema from my youth returned with a vengeance. From my scalp to my feet, my skin itched like crazy. A circular bald spot an inch wide appeared at the crown of my head. It looked like I had cradle cap. I was too embarrassed and in too much pain to venture out. I looked like a burn victim. I had open scratches and painful, tight scabs all over my body; reptilian-looking scales emerged on my face, feet, and hands. We had no air-conditioning in the apartment, and salt from my sweat stung my skin. I gained a lot of weight during my pregnancy and was huge. Large, visible veins surfaced on my enormous breasts.

Because I was pregnant, the doctors would not prescribe the corticosteroids I had used since I was nine years old to help control the itching and spreading. As a result, I suffered deeply, physically and emotionally. I couldn't stand to look at myself in the mirror. I saw my torment as a sacrifice I needed to make to bring a healthy baby into the world.

In October 1983, I went into labor — for twenty-six hours. James ignored my telephone calls. My mother stayed in the delivery room. After the nurse cleaned and wrapped my baby, she walked toward me. My mother stood next to the bed, on my left. The nurse handed my baby to my mother. After a couple of minutes, I said, "Let me hold her." Only then did my mother hand my daughter to me.

Looking at my baby, I felt that I had something to live for. Babies want their mommies. Finally, someone would want me. I had no husband, no job, and no money, but I no longer wanted to die.

My mother and my brother Kirk's wife, Kim, picked me up from the hospital. The elevator was broken — again. Kim carried Mercedes, and, far behind her, I shuffled up the six flights of dark stairs to my parents' apartment. I had had an episiotomy and was barely able to walk, let alone climb stairs.

Ten days after the birth of our daughter, James called and said he wanted to see her for the first time. It was about 6:00 P.M. James lived less than a fifteen-minute drive from our apartment. I changed out of my loose housedress and put on a pair of pants and a blouse. I dressed Mercedes in a fresh pink onesie with a white bib that said I LOVE MY DADDY. Then I waited.

At 8:00 P.M., I called him. No answer. I waited. At 10:00 P.M., I undressed, took my sleeping daughter's bib off, and went to bed.

The next morning, Faye asked, "What time did James come by last night?"

"He didn't come," I said.

"He *didn't*?" she asked, laughing.

I assumed James would call me in the morning. He didn't. That afternoon, I called him.

"What happened yesterday?" I asked.

"Oh," he chuckled. "I'm sorry, I fell asleep."

THE AMERICAN DREAM

I hated every minute of being on welfare. On the first day of each month, nearly every woman — and some men — in the neighborhood lined up outside of the currency exchange building a few blocks from our apartment. Sometimes I waited to pick up my check on the second or the third, when the line — which could stretch for blocks — was shorter. I felt embarrassed and demeaned when I reached the window and asked for my check. When my daughter was about three months old, I got a job through a temp agency. From work, I proudly called the welfare office and told them I had a job.

"You're entitled to a last check," the woman said.

"I don't want it."

A few months later my parents decided to move out of the housing projects. Most of their children lived elsewhere and they thought they could afford a better neighborhood. Cheryl and I still lived at home, but we both had jobs, and I felt relieved. At least Mercedes would not grow up in the same horrible building that I did.

She won't know nuthin' *about living in the projects*, I thought to myself as I carried her down six flights of stairs for the last time.

We moved into a second-floor apartment on 64th and Paulina Street — about five minutes from James's house.

From the day my mother raided my penny jars and gave what I had saved to my sister, I'd wanted to get back into the practice of saving money, so I got a second job and opened a bank account. I did general secretarial work, typing letters and answering phones, from nine to five in a downtown office. Then, from five thirty to nine thirty, I worked as a typist for another company a few blocks away. There was nothing intellectually stimulating or challenging about what I was doing, but I was a single teenage mother pursuing the American dream. I had no idea, however, that that ship had sailed a long time ago.

I tried to keep James in my life, but he rarely came to see me and Mercedes at home. If I said, "James is coming over to see Mercedes," my father would stay in his bedroom until James was gone. "I don't want him in my house," he told my mother. And he refused to speak to him.

When Mercedes was about a year old, we took a bus to James's house. I sat with James in the living room, where we watched TV and talked. Mercedes toddled around, exploring everything. Suddenly James said he had been thinking. He thought maybe we should live together. I told him that I didn't want to do that.

"Well, why don't we just get married, then?" he asked.

"Yes!" I said.

"I don't have a ring, but I'll get you one," he said.

I went home and told my mother that James and I were getting married.

"He didn't give you a ring?" she asked.

"He said he's going to get me one."

A few weeks later, I visited James at his house again. As we sat in his living room, he told me that when he had proposed, he had been "sincere at that moment" but had since decided that it wouldn't work. I responded the way I always did. I sat on his living room sofa, staring my deer-in-the-headlights stare, pretending that I didn't care. Since I had never had any defenders, pretending that I didn't care what people did to hurt me became my ultimate personal defense.

But that was just my reaction in the moment. I wasn't going to work two jobs and raise a daughter alone while James spent money on other women. I hired a lawyer and sought child support. In court, James did not dispute that he was Mercedes's father. The judge ordered him to pay around $200 a month, or $50 a week. He also ordered James to pay me $5,800 in back child support.

James said nothing to the judge. But outside the court, he said, "I can't afford that."

In lieu of weekly payments, James sometimes gave me baby clothes or Pampers. When he was laid off, he stopped doing even that. I went back to court and told the judge that James was not paying court-ordered support, and he placed a lien on James's house. If he ever sold the house, he would be forced to pay everything he owed me for child support, the judge explained. That act drove a wedge between us.

"My house is all I have," he said. "I'll never let you make me lose it."

THE CRIME

I signed on with several temporary agencies. If a job ended, I asked for a new assignment. If nothing was available, I called another company. Often, I worked two jobs a day. After my last shift, I trudged along Chicago's dark downtown streets, caught the El, and headed home. I tried to be as inconspicuous as possible. I didn't want to attract the attention of the kinds of people who rode the El at night. After I got off at 63rd and Ashland, I walked two blocks to the second-floor flat where I lived with my parents and Cheryl. Bone-tired, I would breathe a sigh of relief after I climbed the stairs and turned the key to our front door.

I paid my mother $50 a week to babysit Mercedes. Before I left for work, I closed my bedroom door. It didn't matter. While I was out, my mother moved my things and threw away books and magazines that weren't Jehovah's Witness approved. She tossed them in the dumpster in the alley behind our building, where I wouldn't dig them out.

When I would ask, "Why were you in my room?" my mother would smirk and say nothing.

Juggling jobs wore me down. On the news, recently elected President Reagan promised Americans a new beginning. "In this blessed land, there is always a better tomorrow," he said. I didn't see it. Every morning, I left the apartment in tears while my daughter cried and reached for me, wanting me to hold her. When I finally got home after 10:00 P.M., I ate a sandwich or the day's leftovers. Exhausted, I fell into the twin bed I shared with my daughter.

Mercedes turned two in October 1985. "I'm moving to Milwaukee," I told my mother, and the day I left, my father seemed troubled. He loved Mercedes and would miss her. Perhaps he'd even miss me.

My brother Townsell recruited a friend of his to help me move. I put everything I owned — a crib, a few toys, my clothes, a toothbrush — into his friend's van, and we hit the road, headed for Milwaukee, the place where two of my mother's sisters still lived, and which had been my refuge throughout my childhood. My aunt Amie had driven me home from the hospital after I was born with jaundice. Now she had helped me find an apartment on North 94th Street, a street lined with beige apartment buildings, sidewalks, and neat little squares of lawn.

Mercedes's father wasn't happy about the move and didn't understand why I would move to Milwaukee. "You talk about Milwaukee like it's the best place on earth," James said. He didn't get it. My mother could not poke through my things in Milwaukee, and though we lived just minutes from him in Chicago, he was only visiting his daughter maybe once a month.

I landed a job as a temporary secretary earning $8 to $10 an hour. I also talked to an air force recruiter. My father had been in the air force, and I wanted to feel like I belonged to something. I craved discipline. Also, I thought I would learn to fly. But the recruiter told me that I couldn't be a single mother with sole custody of my child and join the military. Someone else would have to have legal custody of my child in case something happened to me while I was deployed. I didn't want to give up custody of Mercedes, so I didn't join the air force.

My neighbor offered to babysit Mercedes. My aunt knew her, so I trusted her. I needed to work as many hours as I could to pay the rent. One day I came home early. I walked to my neighbor's apartment to get Mercedes, but my neighbor wasn't there. It turned out, she had a day job and had been leaving my daughter with her mentally disabled teenage son while she worked. Usually, she got home just before I did, so I never knew what was going on. She would greet me and act as if she had spent the day with Mercedes.

"I needed the extra money," she explained.

I found a new sitter.

A few months after my move, I returned to Chicago to visit my parents. It was a Sunday, December 15, 1985. I didn't call ahead; I wanted to surprise them.

I packed a bag and some Pampers for Mercedes, and my aunt's boyfriend drove us to the bus station. In Chicago, I took the El to 63rd and Ashland. I carried Mercedes, who had fallen asleep, to my parents' apartment. I knocked, but no one answered. Then I remembered: It was Sunday, and they were probably still at the Kingdom Hall.

No matter, I thought. *We can visit James first.* I knew he would be glad to see Mercedes. I took the 63rd Street bus from Paulina Street to James's house on South Claremont Avenue.

I got off at 63rd and Western and walked back to Claremont. A bitter wind frosted my face, and after two bus rides and a trip on the El, I felt drained and hungry. Plus, I was on my period. I crunched through the snow and ice while carrying Mercedes. Everything looked gray: the low overcast sky, the dirty snow piled up on the ground. The wind cut right through my dark-blue, hooded parka. I could never find a pair of mittens that would keep my hands warm or a pair of earmuffs that would stop my ears from tingling. I had bundled up Mercedes in little white boots, a pink-and-white hat and matching scarf, and a pink two-piece snowsuit with a hood and a loose zipper that I secured with a safety pin. All those clothes made her heavy.

I spotted James's house, a red-brick duplex on a street filled with multifamily homes. He lived with his older sister and her son, two blocks from 63rd and Western, one of the busiest street corners in Chicago. Buses, trains, and taxis rumbled through crowded intersections. All kinds of restaurants, a few grocery stores owned by immigrants, a Sears store, and a big fairly new Jewel-Osco supermarket lined the street, and yet the neighborhood was quiet.

Lugging Mercedes, my purse, and a diaper bag, I climbed the short flight of stairs and rang the doorbell. There was a large picture window on my left, overlooking the porch. I could see figures — a leg, a hand — moving inside. Someone peeked through the curtains, but no one opened the door.

Curious, I sat on the top step for what seemed like a long time. It felt good to put my bags down for a minute. But what was going on in the house?

I waited ten minutes in the cold. But I couldn't leave the neighborhood; I had nowhere to go. My parents would still be at the Kingdom Hall.

I had an irresistible impulse to know who was in the house. James would never make me sit in the cold with our two-year-old daughter. Something must be wrong. A weird feeling washed over me. I felt like I was in a dream. Why didn't he open the door?

"Mama, I cold," Mercedes cried.

I gathered Mercedes in my arms and walked to the Jewel-Osco on 60th and Western. I walked around inside the store to kill time. I bought animal crackers and apple juice for my daughter and a Milky Way bar for myself. I figured I could make a meal later at James's place.

I paid the cashier and walked through the store aisles, feeding Mercedes and eating my candy. I wandered down an aisle jammed with household supplies: can openers, pizza cutters, kitchen knives.

I lingered there. Something was wrong.

A familiar sense of impending danger swirled around me like a fog. Painful memories surfaced, nudging me. I had never felt safe in my life, not for a moment.

I thought I had found a safe harbor with James. I thought Mercedes would be part of a family. It hadn't worked out that way — *yet*, I told myself. A part of me still thought that once James saw Mercedes and we talked, we could start over. Maybe things could still work out.

But not if something terrible happened to him first. I couldn't let that happen. I had to make sure he was okay. I had to get inside that house. Once inside, I might have to fight the person who had first refused to let me in.

I grabbed a butcher knife with a brown plastic handle, paid the cashier, and hurried back to the house.

Yvette — a woman James had once introduced to me as his cousin — finally opened the door. "Come in," she said gruffly, angrily looking me up and down. I sat down on the living room couch facing the large picture window where I'd seen the curtains move. James's bedroom was to my left. He came out of the bedroom and sat on the sofa beside me, to my right. Mercedes stood on the floor in front of us. I took off her coat so that she could warm up. I looked around. The furniture had been rearranged; new pieces had been added. I had spent time in the apartment on earlier visits, but now the layout was unfamiliar. It didn't make sense to me. Yvette asked James if he wanted some tea. "Yes, baby." She passed me and walked down the short hallway that led to the kitchen.

Was James playing a joke on me? I stood up to feel more in control. "Why did you make me and Mercedes wait outside?" I asked him. He said nothing. He wouldn't even look at me. Just like my mother wouldn't look at me when I asked her why she entered my bedroom while I was working. James looked past me and stared out the window as if I wasn't there. Yvette placed a cup of tea on the table in front of the couch.

"Thank you, baby," James said.

"Isn't that your cousin?" I asked.

Derision and pity showed on his face.

For the first time, I noticed there were other people in the house. They had crept into the living room from the kitchen in the back of the house. They stood around, watching me. I didn't know any of them. I was confused. They seemed mysterious — threatening somehow, yet slightly out of focus and dreamlike. Later, I'd discover Yvette and James had been married for two weeks. The strangers in the house were Yvette's friends and family members.

I looked at them, but no one spoke to me. Then I looked back at James. He was looking at me, laughing.

"I'm sorry," he said.

James had humiliated me many times. I had only known him for a few months before I got pregnant. Deep into my pregnancy, he often offered to take me to dinner. Each time, I dressed and waited by the window. He never showed. Silently, I would undress and crawl into bed. He asked me to marry him, then changed his mind. *I was sincere at that moment*, he said.

I went numb. Staring straight ahead, I told myself I was okay.

But I wasn't. At that moment, despite whatever things he might have done, James Francis Bankston became a stand-in for everyone who had ever hurt me, and I had been abused all my life. Yvette represented my siblings, who always seemed to be a part of something that excluded me, siblings who, conspiring together, always made me the butt of a secret joke. The condescending and dismissive smirk on James's face mirrored the look my mother gave me every day of my life. The people in James's house might also have been my siblings, who, standing in our crowded apartment, witnessed my constant, abject misery with amusement and scorn. When I peered into James's bedroom, I saw myself in his bed. It made me feel used. For a moment, James became my brother, who had sexually abused me every day for years.

People say that, when facing danger, our options are fight or flight. Hormones prepare your body to either stay and deal with a threat or to run away. I never had those options. When I tried to fight, my mother defended my abusive siblings and told me to shut up. I was always wrong. Since there was no point in fighting, and there was no place for me to flee, I would freeze. Tonic immobility.

I spent my entire childhood detached from what was happening to me and disconnected from my fear, pain, and sadness.

Not this time. I felt rage at the mocking faces before me. I felt humiliated. I felt angry, embarrassed, a fool, helpless.

I had gone there thinking James could visit Mercedes and we could talk like old times while I waited for my parents to come home. But no one would open the door. Why not? Maybe James needed help, maybe he *couldn't* open the door. I had to get in and find out what was going on.

Now the joke was on me — as always.

"I'm sorry, too," I said.

Still standing, I reached into my purse, grabbed the grocery store knife, and stabbed him in the chest.

James sat on the couch, his feet resting on the sofa table in front of him. The new blade was so sharp his flesh provided no resistance to it. It easily entered his body. I felt angry when I plunged it in and dead inside as I pulled it out.

James briefly winced, looked at me — oddly, the smirk hadn't gone away — and calmly asked me, "What's that?" Then he saw the blade, and a flash of realization crossed his face. He grabbed his cup of tea and threw it in my face.

I was wearing soft contact lenses, and for a moment, I couldn't see. I stumbled back from the couch, away from him.

"Help me, help me, baby, come get this bitch off me!" he yelled.

With my vision clearing, I reached for Mercedes, but she had walked away. The five women in the house came into sharp relief, including Yvette and James's sister, Tina. The other three women stood between my daughter and me. I saw Mercedes, and I froze. She was too young to understand what was happening. She simply stood against a wall in the living room, looking around at everyone.

Time stood still. My head throbbed. I held the knife by its blade, and my right hand was sliced and bloody. The pain was excruciating. From what seemed like far away, I heard Yvette scream. The room filled with noise and movement. Yvette's friends and family members must have been running toward James, but at that moment, I thought they were attacking me.

I ran to the front door and opened it, but the storm door was shut tight. Two people behind me closed the front door, smashing me between the front door and the storm door. I was trapped. Two men came out of the house across the street. I banged on the storm door. "Help me, help me!" I screamed. The two men ran toward the house and tried to open the storm door but couldn't. When they heard police sirens, they ran away.

A patrol car stopped in front of the house. Two white male officers approached, and one of them opened the storm door. I stepped onto the porch. One of the officers pointed his gun at me and told me not to go anywhere. I stared blankly at the gun and then at him. It didn't occur to me to run. My daughter was in that house. I wasn't going to leave her. Plus, I thought the police would help me. The other officer went into the house. I heard a lot of screaming. Then an ambulance arrived. My hands were cut, but the ambulance didn't stop for me. The police handcuffed my bloody hands behind my back and put me in the back seat of the police car. Another woman arrived in a car. She parked with a screech, jumped out, and ran toward the house, screaming, "Who did it? Who did it?" Two EMTs carried James out of the house on a stretcher and placed him in the ambulance. I could see his face. He was alive.

I thought, *He'll be all right.*

I asked the officers, "What about my daughter?"

One of them said, "You can't take her where you're going."

CONFESSION

Two officers took me to an interrogation room in the Eighth District police station. The bare room contained a long table and four chairs. An officer placed a chair near a radiator. "Sit," he said. He cuffed my right hand to a rail along the wall. I could feel the heat from the radiator.

For the next few hours, police officers came and went, asking me if I wanted to make a statement. I told everyone the same thing: "I want to call my parents. They need to get Mercedes." I didn't think about asking for an attorney. Not that I had one to call. I didn't think about asking for a public defender. All I could think about was Mercedes, alone with a bunch of strangers who might take their anger out on her. The only person I wanted to call was my mother. I would take care of everything else once I knew Mercedes was safe.

I told the police officers that my hands were cut up.

"Look at them," I said.

I asked to see a doctor. I told them I needed to go to the bathroom.

"All of that can be arranged after we get your statement," they said.

The officers left the room. Shortly after, photographers took pictures of me and my hands.

Around five o'clock, two police officers came into the room. They uncuffed my hand from the wall. I thought they were taking me to a telephone. Instead, they herded me into the back of a police car and drove me to the Area 3 police station, where they led me to another interrogation room. An assistant state attorney asked me if I wanted to make a statement.

I told him the same thing I told the arresting officers.

"I want to call my parents. They need to pick up my daughter."

"We can take care of that," he said. "But first, we need you to tell us what happened and sign a statement." He said James was in surgery, but he would probably be okay.

"I don't want to sign anything," I said.

"Okay, I'll be back," he said.

Around seven o'clock, the assistant state attorney and a police officer came into the room.

They sat across from me at a long table. One of them wrote my confession on several pieces of paper.

If you sign it, they said, we'll let your mother pick up Mercedes. You can also go to the bathroom and the hospital.

All I could think about was Mercedes. I imagined Yvette and her family and friends doing terrible things to my daughter. I felt sick and hungry. The only thing I had eaten that day was a candy bar. My head pounded. I wore the same sanitary napkin I had worn when I left Milwaukee that morning.

It had been nearly seven hours since I last saw my two-year-old daughter. I signed the papers.

The police officer took me to a desk with a telephone on it. He stood next to me while I called my parents, hoping they would be home. My mother answered. She and my father were eating dinner and watching TV.

"Mama," I said, "I'm in town, and I'm under arrest for stabbing James. I don't know where Mercedes is. You need to go find her."

"Lisa, don't play like that," my mother said.

"No, Mama, I'm not playing."

I turned to the police officer. "My mother doesn't believe me."

He took the phone and told her it wasn't a joke. He told my mother that he could tell that I wasn't a bad person and that I had just gotten caught up in an unfortunate situation.

He handed the phone back to me, and I hung up. The officer uncuffed me and pointed to a bathroom down a short hall. I had to pee really bad by this time. But there were no sanitary napkins in the bathroom. I threw away the one I had been wearing for nearly twelve hours and wadded a bunch of toilet paper and stuffed it in my underwear.

I tried to wash my hands, but they hurt too badly. I had numerous cuts and open slices on my thumbs and palms. I ran water over them and wrapped paper towels around the wounds.

Two male police officers — I had yet to talk to a female officer — stood outside the bathroom. They cuffed my hands when I came out. Then they drove me to a hospital for medical treatment.

A new police officer sat with me in the hospital emergency room. He told me that I should ask the judge to suppress my confession because the detectives had forced me to sign it by withholding medical care. Then he turned to me and quietly said, "You can still be anything you want to be." I stared at him, feeling confused but suddenly hopeful, wanting desperately to believe him. He said, "I've been around a lot of different people, and I can tell that you're a good person."

The assistant state attorney had told me that James would be all right, so I assumed I would be charged with assault and battery. I also thought that the confession would be thrown out.

Later that morning, I was arraigned and charged with first-degree murder. Standing in front of the judge, I blurted out, "James died?" The prosecutor looked at me with surprise — and then he snickered. "Be quiet," the public defender whispered to me.

Surgery had failed to stop James's bleeding, and he had died the next morning. I was thunderstruck. Bail was set at $75,000. I needed $7,500 to get out, but it might as well have been $75 million. I didn't even have $75. I was nineteen, broke, and Black.

COOK COUNTY JAIL

I spent eighteen months in the Cook County Jail in Chicago awaiting trial. Some relatives sent money to my mother to pay for a private attorney, but my well-meaning uncle Henry, a police officer in Milwaukee, told her not to waste the money. A public defender is just as good, he said. She sent the money back.

She never mentioned it to me until after the fact.

If she had, I would have told her that at the jail, the inmates had a nickname for the public defender. The initials *PD*, they said, stood for "Penitentiary Deliverer."

One of the biggest jails in America, the Cook County lockup had housed some of the country's most notorious criminals, including Frank Nitti, Al Capone's henchman, and mass murderer Richard Speck. I slept in a cell with prisoners who were HIV-positive or were huddled on the floor withdrawing from some drug I had never heard of. "Medical emergency! Medical emergency!" the guards screamed while yet another woman seized, thrashed, and urinated on the dayroom floor. "Put something in her mouth so she won't bite her tongue!"

I needed something to do, so I enrolled in a program designed to help prisoners earn a high school diploma. I didn't need one, of course, but I enjoyed talking with the teachers.

During the holidays, entertainers visited the jail. Redd Foxx performed one Christmas season, as did James Brown. Jesse Jackson came to speak. Like the GED classes, these celebrity appearances were welcome distractions, but I was focused on my upcoming trial.

The public defender filed a pre-trial motion asking the court to throw out my forced confession, which I was confident would be deemed inadmissible.

At a pre-trial hearing, I took the stand and testified about my arrest and detainment. Police officers filled the courtroom, and the detectives who arrested me testified. They claimed that I was not in custody for nearly seven hours, although the hospital records showed I wasn't treated until around seven o'clock.

My one hope was my mother's testimony. Initially, she said she would never forget the moment I called her from the police station. The moment would be burned into her memory for the rest of her life, she said. It was a Sunday evening, and they did the same thing every Sunday evening. She and my dad were eating dinner and watching *60 Minutes*, which aired at six o'clock. So she knew it had to be between six and seven o'clock, because that was when *60 Minutes* was on television. But when I asked her to testify to that in court, my father told her that, no matter what she thought, she couldn't really be sure what time it was, and that she shouldn't testify that she could.

So Mama refused to testify on my behalf, even though her testimony would have been crucial to establishing the time that I called.

The judge ruled that the testimony of the police officers was more credible than mine. He also said that he believed I had been to the bathroom at least once prior to signing the confession.

I was dumbfounded.

But all was not lost. My case would go to trial in early 1987, and I was sure a jury would find me innocent. Once I had a chance to explain my lifetime of abuse, they'd understand why I acted as I did.

THE TRIAL

"So, Ms. Forbes, how did it feel to take a butcher knife and plunge it into James Bankston's chest?!" the prosecutor shouted at me.

I had just sat down in the witness chair, having sworn to tell the truth and nothing but the truth, so help me God. I stared at him, frozen. The question hung in the air, unanswered, for what seemed to me like minutes.

I said nothing.

My public defender, Paul Stralka, had given me no preparation for testifying other than to tell me to wear "feminine-looking" clothes. I followed his directions. In my cell that morning, I exchanged my prison uniform for a skirt and a pink blouse.

In his closing arguments, the prosecutor used my attire against me.

"Don't let her sitting here in this ruffled pink blouse fool you," he told the jury in his closing arguments. "If this were a man, you wouldn't hesitate to convict!"

I wore a different outfit every day of the trial — skirts and pretty blouses. At the end of each day, I went straight back to my cell, where I changed and brought my trial clothes to the guard. At some point, my family picked up the dress clothes.

At first, I had been relieved to go to trial, but there were no jurors my age. The youngest were in their thirties or forties. One — an old Black woman — slept off and on during the five-day trial. "Wake her up," the judge repeatedly instructed the bailiff. The jurors were mostly white men, a few of them senior citizens. I didn't see anyone I considered a peer — somebody who might be able to see things from my point of view, someone who had grown up on Chicago's South Side. Looking back, I don't think they saw me at all.

Paul Stralka made no effort to give me a chance to tell my life story, to explain myself, to seek understanding or even context from the jury. He could barely remember my name.

He refused to call my parents to the stand. "What could they testify to?" he asked me. "The jury won't believe anything they say. Of course your family will lie for you."

I didn't understand his logic. The prosecution called James's family to the witness stand. Wouldn't they also be willing to lie for him?

Not a single witness was called in my defense.

Stralka refused to ask the judge to allow the jurors to consider a voluntary manslaughter charge — a strategy I suggested. Instead, he said we should go "all or nothing." When I asked him about potential options for me to avoid prison, such as a suspended sentence, he lied and said, "They don't have that in Illinois."

I urged him to find the two men who heard me scream for help when I was trapped between the storm door and James's front door. They could talk about my state of mind. Stralka assured me those would be good issues to raise on appeal.

On appeal?

During court breaks, the judge allowed me to visit with my family for fifteen minutes. We sat off to the side of the jury box while the jurors were gone. My parents came every day, and I hugged Mercedes during our brief visits. My two brothers never showed. One day my sister Net told me that she had been watching my face throughout the proceedings. "You look like everything is just washing over you," she said. "It's like you're here, but you're not here."

I spent two and a half hours on the witness stand. The jurors took less than an hour to return a guilty verdict. When they were polled, even the old woman who slept through the trial stood up and loudly shouted, "Guilty!"

My reaction was predictable — I just zoned out and went numb. It's hard to say that I lost hope. I didn't feel anything.

Paul Stralka later became a judge.

A few weeks later, a Cook County probation officer interviewed me in jail as part of the court's pre-sentence investigation. The officer planned to send my comments, along with my arrest record — I had none — and my employment history, education level, family situation, and mental health history to the judge handling my case. The information would help the court decide how long I should stay in prison.

The probation officer asked me about my relationship with my family. "Do you get along with your parents, your sisters, your brothers?" he asked.

I didn't want to talk about it.

"It's fine," I said.

He told me he had spoken with Miss Wilson, the eighth-grade schoolteacher who had loaned me books about the Greek gods. "She said wonderful things about you and your skills," he said. But she was confused about why he was calling. She said, "May I ask what this is for?" When he told her that I had been convicted of first-degree murder and that he was conducting a pre-sentencing hearing, Miss Wilson burst into tears and became inconsolable.

After hearing his story, I felt the same way.

He concluded his report by noting that I had "smiling depression."

At the sentencing hearing, the prosecutor introduced a victim impact statement explaining the effects of the killing on James's family, friends, and relatives. Family members took the stand and said they were devastated by his death. He had been a nice and responsible person, they said.

My attorney submitted no such document on my behalf. There was no childhood impact statement to illuminate my mental or emotional health on that terrible day. No one in my family took the stand to argue that I had tried for years to be a nice and responsible person.

Judge Suria sentenced me to twenty-five years in prison.

After my sentencing hearing, the judge allowed me to have a visit in the jury room with my family members who were in the courtroom.

When it was time for them to leave, my uncle Gus burst into tears. I tried to comfort him.

"Don't cry, Uncle Gus," I said. "I'll be all right."

SHIPMENT

About two weeks after my sentencing hearing, hours before dawn, a female guard rapped loudly on my prison door with handcuffs.

"Forbes," she said. "Wake up. You're going on shipment."

I had been in the Cook County Jail for a year and a half.

I walked to the sink and toilet a few feet from the foot of my bed and washed my face and brushed my teeth. My roommate, Brenda, who was HIV-positive, didn't move on the top bunk. She either was asleep or pretended to be. I said nothing.

Instead, I got dressed in my jail uniform, a light-blue pair of pants and a matching short-sleeved pullover shirt. I stripped the sheets and pillowcase off my bed and piled them on the floor next to the cell door. Then I sat on the thin bare mattress, wondering how long it would take for the guard to come back and open the door.

I sat on the bottom bunk with my back straight. The top of my head rubbed against the bottom of the top bunk. I looked up, irritated. That's when I saw it: a lot of my hair was stuck on the rough metal underside of the top bunk.

I'm not superstitious, but for some reason leaving my hair in the Cook County Jail seemed like a bad idea. I grabbed the same towel I had just used to wash my face and began to frantically wipe my hair off the bottom of the top bunk. I looked for other items to clean. I didn't want to leave any part of me behind. The guard came back and opened the door.

"Forbes, time to go."

I dropped the towel on the pile of sheets and pillowcases and kicked the mound into the hallway. The guards would assign someone to clean the area later.

I joined ten other women who were also being shipped out.

"We're going to the big house!" one of them shouted.

A group of guards herded us into the dayroom, where we stood at the door, single file. A lieutenant, a gray-haired Black man, asked each woman, "Name?"

"Lisa Forbes." He checked my name off the list — he never looked at me — and walked to the next prisoner in line.

The door buzzed open, and we hobbled out into the hallway and down three flights of stairs. A lieutenant walked in front of the line, and a guard brought up the rear. On each floor, a new line of chained women joined us. *Shipment* was an appropriate word. I felt like cargo.

Outside, the guards handcuffed me, shackled my feet, and chained me by the waist to the woman next to me. I thought of all the images I'd seen of manacled slaves forced onto ships.

I shuffled toward the bus and struggled to lift my fettered feet high enough to enter. The procession had a dreamlike quality. I felt disconnected from my body and everyone around me. Then, as if from a distance, I heard the other chained women around me. Incredibly, some of them were laughing and joking. I was too numb to cry, but I certainly didn't want to laugh.

A guard on the bus handed each of us a paper bag with a room-temperature sandwich — they swore it was meat — a small carton of lukewarm milk, and a squishy orange. I didn't eat any of it.

After what seemed like hours, the bus approached the Dwight Correctional Center. The maximum-security prison for women was about seventy miles from Chicago, but it might as well have been on a different planet. Prior to my arrest, I had never heard of the village of Dwight, Illinois. All I knew was that I was being taken far from my daughter. I stared out the window, looking at streets and buildings and skylines that I wasn't sure I would ever see again.

"We're here!" one of the prisoners shouted, sounding excited.

The driver pulled up to the prison's gate, which was topped with rings of razor wire. The guards spoke for a couple of minutes. Then the gate opened, and the driver stopped at a small stone cottage inside the compound. Incredibly, the women seemed happy and filled with anticipation. I still felt like I was in a dream. We hopped off the bus, our ankles still chained, and called out our names. A lot of the women had been to Dwight before. They knew the ropes and offered advice.

"How much time you got?" an inmate asked me.

"Twenty-five years," I said.

She looked at me with pity. Then she said she would give me the number of a lawyer who might help me.

We filed into the intake building. A guard removed our cuffs and shackles. A correctional officer led us up a flight of stairs and guided us, two by two, into cells that looked like those at the Cook County Jail. This was Dwight's quarantine area, where they housed prisoners before they were cleared for release into the general population.

For the next week, I underwent a battery of physical and written exams. I saw a doctor, a dentist, a counselor, and a schoolteacher. I took a reading and math test. A psychologist who gave me a multiple-choice test smiled when he read my answers.

"You are atypical," he said.

I didn't ask him what he meant by that.

We stayed locked in our rooms during intake — two inmates to a cell — except for a one-hour recreation break when we gathered in the dayroom to play cards or watch TV. A prison chaplain held services in the evening once a week and on Sunday mornings. Chaplain Barbara Washington, a Black woman in her forties, came by a few times during the week. She stopped at each cell door window and asked the inmates if they needed anything. My answer was always the same. No.

Once we were cleared from intake, we were transferred to the prison hospital, where we waited for a prison official to assign us a security level (minimum, medium, or maximum), a housing unit, and a job. I ended up in medium security because of my long sentence. But I was housed in Cottage 10, with both minimum- and medium-security inmates.

I got a job with the personal property department. I worked five days a week and earned $15 a month cataloging the packages and clothing sent to the women in Dwight. A correctional officer poked over each parcel.

At that time, the women in Dwight could wear their own clothes. If their friends or family sent nothing, they dressed in state-issued light-blue pants, button-down shirts, and a thin navy-blue coat in the winter.

However, prisoners could only receive clothing from home every three years. Most women had their families send them lots of jeans, athletic shoes, and a variety of tops and sweaters. And everyone got at least a couple of outfits to wear during visitation. Usually, they wore a nice dress or skirt, but often they preferred a pair of dress slacks and a pretty blouse.

I had never liked wearing jeans. I loved to dress up. I asked my mother to send me some nice clothes.

"You dress every day like you're going on a visit," an inmate told me.

I got that from my father. When he was younger, he said, he was always the sharpest dresser around. His friends called him Fabulous Forbes.

The personal property department was in the basement of C-10, the building where I lived. I spent all my time indoors. I asked to be reassigned to Leisure Time Services, which provided recreational activities for the inmates. The department supervisor, Edna R. Lee, needed an inmate secretary. I told her I had been a secretary before my arrest, and I had once taken a typing test where I typed a hundred words a minute for five minutes with zero errors. She gave me the job.

Being a secretary afforded me a lot of relative freedom. I helped organize special events, including concerts, the annual inmate 3K race, and Christmas celebrations. I spent a lot of time outdoors. Leisure Time Services also supervised the inmate snack shack in the rec yard. I telephoned vendors and ordered the snack foods. I also met the delivery trucks at the rec yard, unlocked the snack shack, and cataloged the deliveries.

It was considered a plum assignment, and it helped me bide my time until I was released. I had filed my appeal immediately after being sentenced. I was sure a judge would soon overturn my conviction.

I was wrong, of course. Nothing moves quickly in the US court system. In 1989 — two years after I was shipped to Dwight — I finally heard from my newly assigned appellate public defender, Vicki Rogers, who wrote me and said she would handle my appeal. I wrote her a lot of letters. She wrote back, asking a lot of questions. Unlike Paul Stralka, the public defender who had represented me at trial, she seemed genuinely interested in representing me.

Ms. Rogers was confident I would get a new trial. She made me feel good about my chances. "I might even be able to get you out on an appeal bond," she said.

"YOU JUST HAVE TO BE PATIENT"

The appeals court denied my request to leave prison pending my appeal, but my attorney was not discouraged. "Your case remains strong, in part because the original trial judge committed four reversible errors," Rogers said. And my previous attorney had failed to defend me effectively. He had refused to talk to witnesses who might help my case, she said.

It took several months for her to file the brief. After that, we had to wait. Cases were backlogged, she wrote to me.

"Don't worry," she said. "You just have to be patient."

I continued to work as a prison secretary. I participated in the United States Junior Chamber, or Jaycees, program, to learn business and management skills. I slept and ate. At night, I dreamed of my daughter. Although she often wrote to me, Ms. Rogers never visited me in prison.

Three and a half years after I began working with Ms. Rogers, the appellate court rejected my appeal for several reasons.

The detectives who arrested me had said I had the right to remain silent, so I clammed up. That, the appellate judges said, was a mistake. I should have told the investigators I *intended* to remain silent and *then* clammed up. At that point, the police would have stopped interrogating me, but since I didn't announce my intentions, they had the right to keep questioning me for hours. "Defendant could have only ended the interrogation by making an overt response."

They didn't explain how a nineteen-year-old girl would have known that.

The appellate court also ruled that the Chicago Police Department did not act improperly when they interrogated me for several hours while I was injured and bleeding.

Another issue involved jury selection. One of the prospective jurors said that his uncle had been murdered in 1976 in New Jersey. The killers were convicted but released after two years. The juror said he believed that killers should never be set free. He was dismissed, but the public defender worried his remarks might influence the remaining jurors. They might be reluctant to consider a charge of voluntary manslaughter because it would carry a lighter sentence. The judge denied the motion. Instead, he instructed the potential jurors to ignore questions concerning sentencing.

"Your responsibility is to determine whether the state has proved its case beyond a reasonable doubt," he said.

Ms. Rogers was sure the dismissed juror had tainted the jury pool. But the appellate court judges disagreed. The jury's verdict would have been the same no matter what the dismissed juror said, they ruled.

Ms. Rogers lost another argument, too. Before asking them to deliberate, the judge gave the jurors incorrect instructions regarding voluntary manslaughter and first-degree murder convictions. The appellate court rules that the error was harmless because they did not believe it affected the outcome of the trial.

That was the bottom line. None of the things deemed irregular at my trial mattered because I would have been convicted anyway, the appellate court said. For years I thought I would get out. Now, for the first time, I felt hopelessly trapped.

Soon after, Vicki Rogers sent me a letter. It's not over, she wrote. She said she had recently seen my trial judge, Judge Suria, while she was handling a retrial on another case in his courtroom. She had mentioned me, and the judge asked how I was doing. "He seemed to have compassion for your situation," she wrote.

He didn't seem compassionate when he gave me twenty-five years in prison, I said. Was I supposed to be flattered that he remembered me? The judge's interest in my well-being did not lessen my misery — or shorten my sentence. I would spend another twelve or thirteen years in prison.

The appellate court decision came down on October 26, 1990, two days before my daughter's seventh birthday. That's when it hit me: I was not going to see my daughter grow up.

That's when I decided to break out.

TANGO AFTERMATH

My escape plan — climb the prison fence, ignore the razor wire, and escape into the woods — failed miserably. The razor wire slashed my hands, arms, and legs. I fell flat on my back and shattered my left ankle. I dragged myself to the side of the road and called to the first guard I saw.

"I need to go to the hospital," I said calmly. I was a bloody mess, but I felt no pain.

"Did someone attack you?" she asked. I didn't answer.

She looked at my ankle and called for the patrol car. The driver helped me hop on my right leg and into the car. At the prison hospital, another inmate walked over and stared at my left ankle. It bulged over my gym shoe like it was about to explode. "Oh my God!" she screamed. For a second, I thought she was going to faint.

Finally, the nurse came out with a wheelchair.

Warden Jane E. Huch confronted me in the hospital waiting area. A matronly woman with short, graying hair, Warden Huch was hard but fair. She made sure visiting children had plenty of toys. She organized activities in the visiting room so the inmates could get up and play with their children rather than simply sit at tables. I didn't dislike her, but I didn't like her, either. She felt the same way about me. She saw me as different from most of the other inmates. I had spoken with her several times, occasionally striking up a conversation about something that was going on in the world. She would usually find a way to say something about me being "smart." She didn't necessarily dislike me, but she disliked the fact that there was something different in her menagerie.

Unlike the CO, the warden did not assume that I had been attacked. She took one look at me — a woman in a wheelchair with a broken ankle and a bloody jogging suit — and said, "Lisa, you and that fence cannot tango."

I said nothing. I felt light-headed.

The warden and the nurse huddled inside the nurse's adjacent office. I heard the nurse tell Huch, "She's getting kind of shocky." One of the COs handcuffed me. An hour later, a prison van carried me to the emergency room in a hospital in nearby Streator, Illinois.

A male lieutenant CO and two female COs followed me into the hospital's examination room. A nurse cut off my jogging suit and handed the pieces to one of the COs. She cleaned and bandaged the various cuts, bruises, and gashes on my arms, right calf, and thighs. A surgeon, Dr. Sinha, examined my X-rays. He said I cut a tendon in the knuckle of my left ring finger. A nurse pulled up a chair for the doctor. He sat on my left side, in front of the COs and the lieutenant, and placed my left hand on a small table. He put something over his eyes that looked like a magnifying lens, and the COs and the lieutenant leaned in to watch him work. He repaired my tendon and stitched my knuckle together. "You may never again be able to bend that finger," he said.

He stood up and walked to the foot of the bed. "Your left ankle is broken in three places. I'll need to operate. But first I need to reset the joint." He told the nurse to put something in my mouth to bite down on, and he told me to prepare for a sharp pain. I held on to the sides of the gurney and steeled myself. Once again, the COs and the lieutenant inched closer to watch. They approached, wide-eyed, openmouthed, anticipating my pain. A nurse pressed one of her hands on my right thigh and the other on my right calf. Another nurse leaned across my chest and held me down. The doctor grabbed my left calf and pulled down sharply. It was excruciating, but it was over before I could scream. After that, he told the nurse to give me a sedative and take me upstairs into a room. One CO started to cuff my left wrist to the bed. Dr. Sinha said, "That's not necessary. She's not going anywhere." The CO stepped back, and the nurses wheeled me out of the emergency room and into the hallway. As they did so, one CO stayed on each side of the gurney. The lieutenant followed behind.

Once we got to my room, the nurses lifted me onto a regular hospital bed and left. The CO who wanted to restrain me in the emergency room cuffed my right wrist and my right ankle to the bed rail. The two COs stayed overnight, sitting and sleeping in the two chairs in the room.

When Dr. Sinha visited me the next day, he asked if I had any questions.

"Can you perform the surgery with a local anesthetic, so I can stay conscious?" I asked.

He told me that was impossible but that I shouldn't worry.

For the first time, I was terrified. I was deathly afraid of being put to sleep. The doctor seemed nice enough. In fact, one of the COs told me that she had taken her daughter to the hospital when she broke her leg. Dr. Sinha operated on her, she said. I believed her, but it didn't lessen my anxiety. Her daughter wasn't a prisoner. Her daughter hadn't tried to escape from prison, and her daughter wasn't Black. I didn't think they would treat me the same. I did not want to be unconscious at any time. I was afraid that I would wake up without a leg. What better way to make sure that I didn't climb any more fences?

A few hours later, a Catholic priest stopped by to see me. He asked if he could do anything for me. I told him that I was very scared about having to undergo anesthesia. He asked if I had ever been in surgery before. I told him that I hadn't, and I was afraid I would never wake up. He asked me if I wanted him to pray with me; I said yes, and he asked God to give me peace. I appreciated the fact that my being chained to the bed didn't stop him from attempting to comfort me. A nurse gave me a sedative, and I went to sleep.

Dr. Sinha operated on my ankle the next morning. He must have assumed that I had been given a local anesthetic while being prepped for surgery. While I was on the operating table, but still conscious, he walked over and began lightly tracing where he planned to make the incision. Whatever he was using had a sharp edge. I said, "I can feel that." He stopped, looked at me, and put down whatever was in his hand. Then he started rubbing my left ankle with his fingers. He asked, "Can you feel that?" I said, "Yes, I can feel your fingers now, but a minute ago, I felt something sharp." He spoke softly to the anesthesiologist, who then told me to count backward from ten. Staring at the ceiling, I called out numbers. I saw a black curtain form in my peripheral vision on my right side. As I continued to count, the curtain got closer and closer. When I got to five, I immediately changed vantage point, and instead of being on my back and looking up, I was near the ceiling and looking down.

I heard everything the doctors, nurses, and correctional officers said. I saw everything they did.

When I came out from under general anesthesia, I was extremely nauseous. After what seemed like an interminable time of violent vomiting, a nurse came and wheeled me from recovery back to my room.

While there, I described everything that had gone on during the operation to prove that it wasn't a dream or a hallucination.

The correctional officers who stayed at the hospital while I was there rotated as their shifts changed. During my surgery, Lieutenant Armstrong, one of the correctional lieutenants from the prison, was present. While I was under anesthesia, I heard her tell the other correctional officers in the room, "She thinks she's better than other people." Afterward, I told Lieutenant Armstrong what I heard during surgery.

"You said I think I'm better than other people." She stared at me and said, "Oh, you heard that, did you?" Then she walked away and sat in a chair near the door.

Later that afternoon, Dr. Sinha visited me. He asked me how I was feeling. I said, "Dr. Sinha, I want to tell you something. I wasn't asleep during the surgery. I wasn't in any pain, but I wasn't asleep." He looked at me like he didn't understand me. I didn't want to tell him what I'd heard Lieutenant Armstrong say, so I told him a different story from my time under anesthesia.

After the surgery, my jaw had clenched. Dr. Sinha had massaged my jaws and tried to get them to relax so he could open my mouth. At this point, I was back in my body. I could see him even though my eyes were closed. I could hear him, and I knew exactly what he wanted me to do. But I couldn't move. The anesthetic had induced paralysis and analgesia, but not unconsciousness. One of the nurses said he needed a crowbar, and everybody laughed. Dr. Sinha chuckled while he continued to try to loosen my jaws. A moment later, I surrendered to a brief period of unconsciousness.

I described to Dr. Sinha what had occurred with my jaws in the operating room and I repeated the nurse's joke. I told him I had watched them work on my body. It was as if the anesthesia had forced me out of my body, but I hovered over it until I could get back in. He gasped and stared at me as if he was stunned. I reassured him that I had not suffered or felt pain during the operation. I simply never lost awareness. He seemed genuinely relieved.

Equally important to me was that he didn't dismiss my story as some kind of hallucination. He believed me.

Dr. Sinha had inserted pins into my ankle. He warned me that I might limp for the rest of my life. After three days in the outside hospital, I was discharged and taken back to prison. The hierarchy among the correctional officers consisted of officers, sergeants, lieutenants, and captains. It seemed like someone in each rank was surrounding me when I got back to Dwight. Two African American male captains with Jheri curls carried me down a flight of stairs to the basement of the administration building, where I got a new ID card. I had not been allowed to comb my hair during my three-day stay in the hospital; it stood wildly all over my head.

One of the captains who had carried me down the stairs, a Black man, motioned to my hair and told a CO, "Let her comb her hair."

But nobody gave me a comb. My ID identified me as an extremely high escape risk. I was the only prisoner in Dwight who had ever been issued a high-risk green card. With my tangled, uncombed hair, the new photo made me look like a crazy person.

RECOVERY

The prison had two areas for solitary confinement, or what it called segregation. One was a separate unit of segregated inmates, which was one half of the cottage where maximum security inmates were housed. The other was a segregated section of the prison hospital. The warden placed me in a segregated cell in the prison hospital. The surgeon at the outside hospital had prescribed crutches for me to get around. No one delivered them.

Warden Huch came to see me. "Lisa, I know how you feel."

"No, you don't."

"Okay, so I don't. But I do know that it's going to be harder on you because you're smart."

A few days later, she authorized the COs to give me crutches. I was grateful. They made it easier for me to get from the bed to the toilet. Up until then, I had been hopping on my right leg to move around.

I wasn't allowed a TV or radio in seg, and I couldn't wear my own clothes. Instead, I had to wear an ugly yellow jumpsuit. But I could receive books through the mail. I wrote to friends, acquaintances, and strangers and asked them for things to read. I piled books on my bed and leaned them against the three walls of my cell.

Mostly, the COs left me alone. Since none of them were blamed for my attempted escape, most didn't think it was necessary to take it upon themselves to punish me.

The inmate workers at the hospital didn't bother me, either. I thought most of the inmates secretly sympathized with me. In fact, a story about my escape circulated in the prison. In the inmates' version, I had tried to escape because somebody was abusing my child. I had to rescue her. Most of the inmates were mothers and sympathized with me. I didn't dispute the prison version.

My first months were hard. I had wrecked my body and was facing a year of isolation.

I created a routine to help me make it through.

Breakfast, served on a three-sectioned Styrofoam plate, often included something runny: oatmeal or biscuits and gravy. Sometimes a CO would deliver my meal, open my cell door, and ask if I wanted coffee. Other times the kitchen workers would deliver the meal. Because the kitchen workers couldn't unlock the door, they had to fold the Styrofoam plate and quickly shove it sideways through the bars to keep everything from running out. On those days, breakfast was an unrecognizable, soggy mess. But it seldom mattered to me. I hardly ever ate breakfast; if it came with a piece of fruit, I would save the fruit for later. Sometimes breakfast would be powdered eggs. If the eggs were still warm (they were never hot), I would eat them along with a biscuit and a pack of grape jelly. I would always drink the coffee. If the CO didn't delay in bringing it, the coffee would be reasonably hot and I enjoyed a hot cup of coffee in the morning. I would ask for two packs of cream (a pack of lumpy nondairy creamer) and two packs of sugar. Sometimes they would give me extra for later. Occasionally I got two cups of coffee, an act of kindness.

When I was done, I slid the Styrofoam plate and cup through the bars and set them on the floor to be picked up by the "housegirls" — inmates who were assigned to keep the hospital clean. Most of the housegirls lived in the hospital, because they were either sick or pregnant and close to their due date. They were not in segregation.

After breakfast, I'd pick up a book to read. I broke large books into sections or chapters, and, acting like a teacher, I'd assign myself an amount to read each day. I would read and study until lunchtime. After lunch, I would either write letters or continue reading. I wanted to keep a journal, but I worried the COs would confiscate it and read it.

Dinner, delivered between 5:30 and 7:00 P.M., provided an occasional break from isolation. Three times a week, the CO allowed me to sit in a small dayroom near my cell and eat my dinner there. Often another officer, sergeant, or lieutenant would be patrolling the hospital around that time, and they would linger to chat with me. They talked about current affairs, the news, or a movie they had seen, and sometimes we even discussed a book I was reading. It was a relief to talk about things that had nothing to do with prison. I discovered *Transcendental Meditation* by Robert Roth in the small bookshelf in the hospital dayroom. I couldn't sit cross-legged with a cast on my leg, so I sat on my bed with my right leg bent, but my left leg stretched out in front of me. The practice calmed me, reduced the pain in my ankle, and helped me to ignore the incessant itch beneath my cast.

After about three months, Warden Huch allowed me to buy a radio from the commissary. When I didn't feel like reading, I would lie on my bunk and tune it to the stations that played pop music from the '80s. I listened to a lot of Janet Jackson. I loved her romantic love song "Let's Wait Awhile" with the line in which she tells her lover she'll never give up on them.

Every day in my cell — sometimes in the morning, but always before I went to sleep at night — I would lie on my bed and imagine my ankle surrounded by a blue light that would heal it. In my mind, I would try to see myself walking on a beach. At first, I couldn't do it. Then one day, I successfully imagined myself walking. When I could see myself walking in my mind, I knew my ankle was completely healed. I was in a cast for four months. When I went back to a civilian hospital for the last time, Dr. Sinha stared at my X-rays for what seemed like forever. He shook his head repeatedly. Then he walked over to me and gave me a big, long hug in front of the correctional officers. My ankle had healed flawlessly, he said. He wanted to show the X-rays to his students as an example of a perfect healing. My joint had been dislocated, and my anklebone had broken in three places. Yet if not for the screws on both sides of my ankle, it would be impossible to tell from the X-rays that I had ever been injured. My ankle was stronger than ever.

Dr. Sinha used a saw to cut the cast off my calf. The vibration tickled the sole of my left foot. I laughed so hard and long that the officers monitoring me started laughing, too. I couldn't remember the last time I had laughed, and it felt good. Dr. Sinha wished me luck, and a nurse gently removed as much of the loose, dead skin from my left calf as she could.

I took a long look at my outstretched legs.

The bones had healed, but raw red rings encircled both ankles where the shackles had rubbed off the skin. My feet and ankles were badly swollen. A three-and-a-half-inch scar covered my inner left ankle. Fifteen cross-hatched stitch marks appeared on each side of the incision. The stitch marks — all thirty of them — had turned into thirty raised keloids. Each one was itchy, inflamed, angry, and weeping. After four months in a cast, my left calf was little more than a bone covered with blackened dead skin that shed in chunks. A one-inch jet-black bruise spread on the inside of my right calf. In the center of the bruise, a circular plug of flesh was missing. The surrounding tissues wept. An almost identical circular wound oozed fluid from the center of my inner left thigh. My right inner thigh had suffered two diagonal gashes, each about a quarter inch long.

I had always prized my Tina Turner legs. No more. Now I'd be embarrassed to wear a skirt.

Sergeant John Dronenberg put shackles around what was left of my ankles. I was escorted out of the doctor's office and into the prison van. I walked up the steps to the front door of the prison hospital. Once inside, I was escorted to my room. I sat down on my bed, and Sergeant Dronenberg removed the leg shackles and handcuffs.

After he left the room, I continued to stare at my legs. I couldn't get over how different my left leg looked from my right. Razor-wire scars marked my hands and arms. I could never wear a dress or a short-sleeved blouse again.

Two months later, I was handcuffed, shackled, strip-searched, dressed in a prison uniform, and placed in a prison van. A lieutenant and a sergeant rode with me to the Livingston County Courthouse in Pontiac, Illinois, where I faced three to ten more years in prison for my botched escape.

I knew it would be silly for me to ask for a jury trial. So, when the prosecution offered me a three-year sentence in exchange for a guilty plea, I took it. I stood before a judge in a small courtroom, shackled and surrounded by COs. "Guilty," I said. There were no spectators. My chains rattled as I walked. The judge added three years to my twenty-five-year sentence. Under Illinois law, I was required to serve half of that sentence, and then I could be paroled. That meant I would spend at least fourteen years in prison. I was nineteen when I was arrested for murder. I would spend my twenties and early thirties behind bars. Best-case scenario: Mercedes would be sixteen when I got out.

Back at the prison, a young African American sergeant tenderly threw his hand around my shoulder as he escorted me back to the hospital. "Can I tell you something? You can run, but you can't hide."

Emotionally devastated and in pain from the raw skin around my ankles, I recognized that he meant to be kind. But I wasn't in the mood for platitudes. I ignored him and limped into my cage. Sitting on my bunk, I felt the hard metal of the frame through the skinny mattress.

I looked at my legs and arms and cried. My inner forearms had weeping lacerations. The skin on my left ankle looked like a railroad track. I was nothing but scars.

THE EDUCATION OF LISA FORBES

I refused to leave my cell when my one-year isolation ended because I didn't want to have to deal with other inmates, and the warden gave me another thirty days in seg. That worked for me. In fact, I did the same thing a few more times. Finally, a year and a half after my escape attempt, I moved back into the general population. I had enjoyed the solitude and relative peace I found in solitary confinement. Now I slept in a cottage with a lot more people and a lot more noise.

Worse, I was still classified as an extremely high escape risk. If I had to go somewhere, a patrol car ferried me. Even when I was permitted to walk, I never walked alone. Guards escorted me everywhere. A patrol car followed me, or a CO walked beside me. I couldn't walk in line with the rest of the inmates, either, even though we were going to the same place. I walked either ahead of the line or behind. I wore a green ID card — my scarlet letter. Blending in was now impossible.

I no longer dreamed of breaking out. But I found other ways to escape. Now a part of the general population, I could get lost in the bookshelves in the prison library at Jane Addams Hall, a building named after the nineteenth-century Chicago feminist and reformer. Jane Addams Hall quickly became my favorite place. Once a week, I walked down a long hall, passing classrooms on either side, to the school administrator's office, the law library, and the prison library. Although they stood on opposite sides of the same room, the library and the law library were separate. Each required a different pass; being caught in the wrong place could result in a ticket for "unauthorized movement."

The librarian sat at a desk just inside the front door. She was a big woman with pale smooth skin, a youthful round face, and messy, short gray hair. She wore glasses that were even thicker than mine and must have weighed four hundred pounds. Because of my high-risk ID, she watched every move I made.

I could check out five books at a time and renew them as often as I liked. There were no late fees, but a lost book resulted in a ticket, which could result in the revocation of library privileges for thirty days.

I never lost a book. Instead, I collected them. I got books from the library, visitors, pen pals.

"She has more books in her cell than there are in the library," the COs quipped.

In prison, I read the books I could never open as a Jehovah's Witness: *The Complete Works of William Shakespeare, Man's Search for Meaning* by Viktor Frankl, *Crime and Punishment* by Fyodor Dostoyevsky, *The Prince* by Niccolò Machiavelli, and *Moby-Dick* by Herman Melville. I studied the books I thought universities taught, although I had never gone to college. I read books by Black authors, too: *The Bluest Eye* by Toni Morrison, *Things Fall Apart* by Chinua Achebe, *The Autobiography of Malcolm X* by Alex Haley, *Their Eyes Were Watching God* by Zora Neale Hurston, and *Revolutionary Suicide* by Huey P. Newton.

Mark Twain became my favorite author. I loved his irreverent book *Letters from the Earth.* In it, Satan writes a probing letter to his fellow archangels about the inconsistencies of human faith. Twain's writings challenged my beliefs about the world. He took a subject and turned it inside out and upside down.

For years I had been shackled to the religious stories and articles published in the *Watchtower* and *Awake!* magazines. They chronicled a world on the brink: nuclear weapons, child prostitution, drug abuse, school violence, rising delinquency rates, the collapse of the American family. Families are coming apart at the seams! the authors warned.

Twain broke their hold on me. "Sanity and happiness are an impossible combination," he said.

I was like a sponge. For the first time in my life, I could read whatever I wanted — and I had the time to do it.

Malcolm X had taught himself to read and write in prison by copying the entire dictionary, page by page. I followed his lead. I read the dictionary, writing down words I didn't know. I heeded L. Ron Hubbard's advice: "When reading a book, be very certain that you never go past a word you do not fully understand."

I didn't limit my education to books. I still listened to Janet Jackson, but now I also listened to Beethoven, Bach, and Mozart on a Walkman I bought from the prison commissary. Although I had never been a television fan, I purchased a small color TV and watched PBS, where I discovered self-help gurus and spiritual advisers like Wayne Dyer and Deepak Chopra.

I read newspapers, too. My father had always read the *Chicago Tribune*. But the prison library subscribed to lots of papers, from the *Chicago Sun-Times* to local newspapers from Livingston County, where the prison was located. In a pile of old magazines I read an article about politicized prisoner John Perotti's effort in Ohio to organize prisoners into the IWW as state employees. I wanted in. I joined the IWW and was considered a member of the Chicago General Membership Branch in 1990. That's when a man named Michael Stanek began work as office manager at IWW HQ after his release from Terre Haute Federal Prison Camp, where he'd served time from May to November 1989. We became pen pals, and then he started visiting me monthly.

I also met Gary Cox through the IWW. He lived in Colorado but visited me about once a year — sometimes twice.

I wrote opinion letters to the IWW newsletter. Newspapers

printed my letters about prison conditions and the criminal justice system, and strangers wrote me after reading my opinions. A European man working on a documentary on prisons in America visited me in jail. He interviewed me in the visiting room while a two-man camera crew filmed us. I felt like I was helping to shed light on the dark corners of the American prison system. Afterward, he told me I was an educated and cultivated woman.

"I am sorry you are in prison," he said.

I took college courses, too. I had taken a few correspondence courses before my escape attempt. After that, I began to take classes taught by a handful of teachers at Lewis University, a private Roman Catholic college in Romeoville, Illinois. I relied on Pell Grants to afford tuition at the school, named by *US News* and the Princeton Review as a top Midwest university. I took classes on ethics, the federal government, microeconomics, sociology, preparatory analysis, algebra, geometry, and Western civilization. Most of the classes were held on weekday evenings in Jane Addams Hall in rooms where the inmates studied for their high school diplomas during the day. Between ten and fifteen students attended each class.

Mr. Drilling, a former radio broadcaster, taught economics and ethics. His deep, resonant voice was authoritative and soothing. I owned nothing, but microeconomics appealed to my interest in logical thinking, how people responded to incentives, and how they faced trade-offs. I was drawn to the concept of "opportunity cost," the idea that the cost of something is what you give up to get it. You could sell a stock and make a quick profit — but you would also lose any gains the investment might earn in the future. The idea guided me in my prison life. What would my future actions cost me? Would the benefit outweigh the cost?

Since I rarely had a cellmate, it was easy for me to study and do my homework at night and on weekends. I wrote in bed or at a small metal table with a metal pull-out seat under a steel-grated window. My hard work paid off. In the early 1990s, I made the Dean's List.

I took more classes in vocational math, desktop publishing, computerized accounting, and computer technology and computer programming. I stayed on the Dean's List.

I took a computer programming class almost by accident. One day the instructor, Mr. Alan Mortensen, saw me in the library typing up a homework assignment for another class. He stood behind me. My typing speed intrigued him. I was fast, and I made few, if any, mistakes. He introduced himself and asked if I would be interested in taking his computer class. I enrolled, and it became one of my favorites. I loved computer programming for the same reason that I loved math. Everything was logical. The "truth" of a program didn't depend on what others thought. It wasn't subjective. What I wrote either produced the desired result or it didn't. I craved that kind of order and control. Because I was good at programming, I thought I might work as a computer programmer, although I didn't pick classes that I thought might help me land a job one day. Instead, I studied everything. I was mentally hungry, and there was nothing else to do. I didn't hang out with the other women. I didn't watch MTV or *Cops*. I read and studied to pass the time.

In May 1994, the prison held a graduation ceremony in the visiting room. I earned an applied science in computer technology degree, a paralegal certificate, and a computer data technology certificate. A year later, I received degrees and certificates in the fields of commercial art and photography. I also earned a Literacy Volunteers of America certificate and tutored other inmates in reading, math, and English as a second language. By the mid-1990s, I had taken nearly every class that was available.

I wrote a poem in my creative writing class. The instructor, a Black woman in her forties who wore loose flowing clothes and dreadlocks, called our group Chrysalis.

"I think of Dwight as a cocoon," she said. "One day you will emerge from that cocoon and spread your wings like butterflies."

We met on Saturday afternoons in the solarium, a large, window-filled meeting room on the second floor of the prison hospital. The solarium had two long, wooden conference tables and soft, swiveling chairs with black padding. The instructor asked us to write a poem about something in the room. I saw a thermostat and thought of the warden. I wrote:

> *Thermostat is in control.*
> *She determines whether everyone is hot or cold.*
> *She has such an important job,*
> *She fails to realize she doesn't turn her own knob.*

THE PARABLE OF THE ENLIGHTENED MAN

The first book I read in prison was Huey P. Newton's 1973 autobiography. When I picked up the book, I assumed it would simply be Huey Newton's life story. I was astonished by how little I had been taught about the Black Panthers. I had no idea that the Black Panther Party for Self-Defense had created more than sixty community social programs — later renamed Survival Programs in 1971 — under Newton's leadership. They sponsored the Free Breakfast for Children Program and provided shoes and health care for the needy in the Black community. In addition to feeding schoolchildren, the party started People's Free Food Programs, delivering groceries and encouraging community members to vote. They also started a "medical self-defense" program with the creation of health care clinics and their own free ambulance services. Children's development centers, free clothing, free busing to prisons so people could visit their incarcerated loved ones, free housing cooperatives — their list of accomplishments went on and on. My mouth hung open as I read this book. It changed my expectations about what a community program was really supposed to be doing for the community.

Newton, a co-founder of the Black Panther Party, opened *Revolutionary Suicide* with a terrible statistic. The suicide rate for young Black men, he said, had doubled in fifteen years and had become higher than the suicide rate for young white men. Why was this so? Newton echoed the sociologist Émile Durkheim, who argued that all types of suicide are related to social conditions, not individual temperament.

Young Black men, Newton said, had been deprived of human dignity, crushed by oppressive forces, and denied their right to live as proud and free human beings. Millions of Black people had experienced a spiritual death in the United States. "This death is found everywhere today in the Black community," he said. Few could overcome such oppression. "If a man rises up against a power as great as the United States, he will not survive," he said. The result? Many Blacks had been driven to a spiritual death, lapsing into lives of quiet desperation. "Yet all the while, in the heart of every Black man and woman, there is the hope that life will somehow change in the future." But, he added, that change cannot happen without "an assault on the Establishment."

Newton fascinated me. He carried law books in his car. Sometimes, when a policeman harassed someone, Newton read portions of the penal code in a loud voice to the police and bystanders. If a cop took someone to the station, he and the Panthers paid their bail.

Intrigued, I read another of Newton's books, *To Die for the People*, a first-person account of the struggle for Black empowerment in America. I contacted organizations that sent books to prisoners and asked them to send me similar works. I scoured the prison library. No book was too ponderous, academic, or radical. I devoured *The Philosophy and Opinions of Marcus Garvey*, *The Wretched of the Earth* by Frantz Fanon, *The Confessions of Nat Turner* by William Styron, *Africa Must Unite* by Kwame Nkrumah, *Message to the Blackman in America* and *The Fall of America* by Elijah Muhammad, and *Malcolm X Speaks*. I even read *Mein Kampf*, which, oddly, was on the bookshelf in the prison library.

Malcolm X had a lot to say about politics and power, but his statement on prison and reading impressed me more: "I have often reflected upon the new vistas that reading opened to me," he said. "I knew right there in prison that reading had changed forever the course of my life. As I see it today, the ability to read awoke in me some long dormant craving to be mentally alive."

I understood that craving. In prison, I was exposed to a broader world than the one I encountered at home and in Chicago's broken public schools. For me, the prison library was a buffet. I was a prisoner, yet I was free, finally, to read anything I wanted. I sampled everything. If I liked an author, I came back for seconds.

In prison, I met and developed a genuine friendship with Alicia Rodríguez, a member of the Fuerzas Armadas de Liberación Nacional (FALN), a Puerto Rican paramilitary organization that set off 120 bombs in the United States. She was serving a sentence of fifty-five years for seditious conspiracy and other charges. She was warm and friendly, and her conversations were interesting and stimulating. Out of respect, I never asked her about her crimes, and she never asked me about mine. But when I discovered she had been denied parole earlier, I urged her to take a different approach.

"At your next hearing, you should tell the parole board you are sorry for what you did. You should cry. Then you can get out, go home, and go about your business," I said.

"No," she said. "I'm not going to say I'm sorry when I'm not. I have no regrets. I'm a revolutionary."

Because I had a determinate sentence, I had no parole board hearings. The law required me to serve half of my twenty-eight-year sentence. Eventually, President Bill Clinton pardoned Rodríguez and other members of the revolutionary group. He got a lot of flak for it.

I experimented with different lifestyles. I was vegetarian for three years, but eventually I started eating meat again. Being a vegetarian in prison meant the kitchen replaced every meat with a slice of American cheese. Frankly, I was just hungry.

I practiced transcendental meditation, listened to Bob Marley, and played bid whist.

I dove into the world's religions, too. I read the Holy Bible, examined Buddhism, and studied holy Hindu Scripture in the Bhagavad Gita. I would talk religion with anybody — except the Jehovah's Witnesses who conducted Bible studies at Dwight. In search of esoteric knowledge, I signed up for a three-year correspondence course with the Rosicrucians. I also met with a rabbi once a week. I investigated Scientology, completed their *Self Analysis* extension course, and read *Dianetics: The Modern Science of Mental Health* by L. Ron Hubbard. A local Scientologist and his wife came to visit me. We sat in the visiting room, and they told me how Scientology had changed their lives for the better.

No one doctrine appealed to me more than another. If anything, I thought the world's religions shared plenty of creeds, beliefs, and stories. Yet they all claimed that their beliefs were the *true* beliefs. They denounced the followers of other faiths. I thought, if God allows you to treat someone else badly, that's not really God. Nothing I read changed my basic belief.

My search for meaning included orthodox Islam. I observed the fast during the month of Ramadhan (along with the other inmates who attended Muslim services). The prison accommodated our need to eat breakfast before sunrise and dinner after sunset. They delivered our meals to our cottages.

I read the Holy Qur'an during the month of Ramadhan. One story about Moses and a wise man intrigued me. In the story, Moses asks permission to travel with an enlightened man. The wise man worries that Moses will lose patience with him, but Moses promises to be patient and obey him on their journey.

As they travel together, the man does things that Moses does not understand. They get into a boat. When they disembark, the wise man makes a hole in the boat so that it will sink. Later they meet a young man, whom the enlightened man kills. Finally, they arrive at a town where the townspeople refuse them food. As they leave, the enlightened man builds up the crumbling wall surrounding the town.

Each time Moses is aghast. Explain your actions, he pleads.

The wise man agrees. Why did he damage a boat owned by poor people on the river? Because a greedy king in a nearby town was about to seize it.

Why did he kill the young man they met on the road? Because the irreligious man would have likely instilled disbelief in his faithful parents.

And the wall? Why did the wise man alter it? It belonged to two orphan boys in the city. Under it was a treasure that belonged to them.

The two men part ways. "I did not do any of this of my own bidding," the enlightened man says. "This is the true meaning of things."

I loved that parable. It made me think of my own life. Even though my boat had a hole in it, perhaps there was a reason it was sinking. Maybe it would lead to something good. There was another message, too. No one person can know everything. The need to understand the world is ongoing.

OF THEE I SING

During my year and a half in segregation, I had no bunkmates, just three walls, a barred door, and a grated window. I had a lot of time to think about the prison, myself, society, and the world.

One day I started writing. I wrote in spurts — at night, in the morning, whenever I tired of reading — with a blue ballpoint pen on a yellow legal pad from the commissary. I started explaining the world to myself; I called that explanation "Of Thee I Sing: Africans in the Land of the Free." After quoting the Declaration of Independence and the Bible, I wrote the first sentence.

"No one can continuously control another human being, without the permission of the one being controlled. That is the most closely guarded secret in the world, for within it lies the foundation of true freedom, and it is the key to the demise of every oppressive government in the world."

I was spurred, in part, by a startling prediction by a social observer. Before the end of the century, he said, roughly 70 percent of all African American males will end up as prisoners, addicts, crazy, or dead.

How could such a thing happen? I asked.

I remembered an old saying: When men try to topple a tree, a hundred men hack at the bark or branches while one man digs at the roots. I wanted to get at the heart of what was happening in America. I used the example of a school bully to explain it. The bully's victims are often smaller, weaker, and fearful, I wrote. I called the bully Willy and his victim Billy.

"Now every day, when he gets the urge, Willy kicks Billy in the seat of his pants. And every day, Billy runs home crying. The respective parents, having held a conference between themselves, forbid Willy to kick Billy and encourage Billy to forgive Willy. So he does. And on the way home from school the next day, Willy beats the stuffin' out of Billy. What is the solution to his problem . . . another parent conference? That has already failed. The obvious solution is that Willy must learn that Billy will not accept being kicked and beaten, and the only person who can effectively teach him that is, of course, Billy himself. The simple fact is that if someone kicks you once, it is his responsibility, but if someone kicks you all the time, the responsibility is yours, because you have then taught him that he can kick you without repercussion. If you let him do it day after day and only cry or complain about it, without really doing anything to force him to stop it, what message have you really given him? Namely, this: that although you will complain, he can nevertheless continue doing the thing he likes to do . . ." Why is that? Because the bully pays no real price for his crime.

I continued. Minorities, in particular, can identify with the victim Billy. All people of color are called minorities, I wrote. According to *Webster's Dictionary*, the root of the word *minority* is "minor," which is an adjective meaning "less; inferior in importance of degree; inconsiderable." Thus minorities are defined as "the party of smaller numbers." Who claims to be the majority? Caucasian men. But how can that be when more than 80 percent of the world's inhabitants are people of color? "Words have meanings, those meanings have effects, and often that effect upon us works at the subconscious level," I wrote. "All of our harassers — be they physical, emotional, sexual, chemical, financial, legal, or otherwise — require fearless confrontation before they can be overcome."

No topic was taboo in my free-ranging dissertation: Black history (Africans have worn throughout history more crowns and jewels than chains); the negative connotation of the word *black* (blackball, blackmail, black market, black sheep, blackguard); capitalism (rule by the rich); and brainwashing.

"Adolf Hitler is reported to have said that people can be made to believe anything if they are told it often enough and if they are told nothing else. This concept is called The Big Lie."

I wrote about prisons, of course, and the striking similarities between prison and slavery. In 1796, I noted, New York lawmakers voted to free the state's African slaves. They also voted to build the state's first prison. "Coincidence?" When I wrote "Of Thee I Sing," Black inmates made up more than half of all prisoners in the US, even though they made up less than 15 percent of the population.

I studded my paper with quotes, including this one from William James, the nineteenth-century American philosopher and psychologist: "The greatest discovery of my generation is that men can alter their lives by altering their attitudes of mind."

BAPTISM

Dwight Correctional Center was the only prison in the state of Illinois without a chapel. But after a decade of fundraising by Church Women United in Illinois, officials added a chapel in 1993. I attended church services of all kinds. Like many of the women there, I sometimes signed up for church services simply to escape the confines of our prison cottage. And sometimes, I enjoyed them. Barbara Washington, the Black chaplain, often held evening prayer services. Although Chaplain Washington preached at some church services, she didn't preach during the prayer services. Instead, we gathered in small groups, and everyone prayed as the spirit moved them. It was common for some of the women, along with Chaplain Washington, to pray in tongues. One evening I prayed out loud in English. I asked God, as I often did, to put a "hedge" around Mercedes to protect her while I was in Dwight. I wanted Mercedes to have a safe and happy childhood. Suddenly, for several minutes, a stream of strange words flowed from my mouth. Unbidden, I was speaking in tongues myself. Afterward, I felt a great sense of calm and peace.

My parents and Mercedes rode a bus provided by the Illinois prison system to Dwight each month. One day we sat at a table in the visiting room. "Mercedes is going to get baptized," my mother announced.

I objected strenuously.

"Mercedes can't get baptized as a Jehovah's Witness," I said. "She's only thirteen! She's too young to make a decision that she'll have to live with for the rest of her life."

If Mercedes made a mistake and the church elders banned her from the larger group, she would suffer the way I had as a teenager. Family members who were Jehovah's Witnesses — including my parents — would not be allowed to speak to her or associate with her. I was desperate to protect her from their harshness.

I wanted Mercedes to wait until I was released before she made such a life-changing decision. She would be eighteen then. If she still wanted to get baptized, I would fully support her decision.

"Well, this is what she wants to do," my mother said.

"What do you mean, this is what she wants to do? Mercedes is a minor, and I'm her mother!" I said. "I feel like you're rushing to get her baptized before I get home!"

"Well, what would you do if you were home?" my father said, looking at my mother and chuckling.

She snickered and looked at me.

"This is wrong," I said. "Mercedes is my child, not yours."

My mother laughed. "Well, there's nothing you can do about it."

Mercedes sat silently, looking first at me and then at her grandparents.

I felt utterly betrayed. My parents had never respected my wishes. They cut short their visit and left.

After that, they rarely visited me.

Eventually the warden changed my status from "extremely high escape risk" to "high escape risk." I exchanged my green ID card for a red one. I was allowed to work in the prison commissary. A few years later, I was deemed a "medium escape risk," which came with a blue ID card. I was transferred from Dwight Correctional Center to spend the last eighteen months of my sentence in the co-ed Dixon Correctional Center in Dixon, Illinois.

In Dixon, I enjoyed the same freedoms as the other female prisoners. That was just about the only thing I liked about my new home. The Dixon guards — especially the women — blatantly favored the male prisoners. If male and female inmates were caught passing "kites," or notes, the COs punished only the women.

I had much less privacy in Dixon. I slept in a room with seven other women occupying four bunk beds. As a result, I didn't read as much. Still, I recognized that my transfer was a sign that my time behind bars was winding down. So I focused on my post-release plans — I wanted to work and reconnect with my daughter — and stayed to myself.

HOME

On December 30, 1999 — my "out date" — I left prison. I exchanged my navy-blue prison uniform for a pair of jeans, gym shoes, a sweater, and a winter coat. My hair was a mess. I combed it straight back, but I had no band to tie it into a ponytail. I didn't care. I just wanted out.

I carried a toothbrush, toothpaste, soap, deodorant, and a small jar of Vaseline in a trash bag. I had packed a few belongings into boxes the day before, and the guards had moved them to the prison entrance: a TV, my Walkman, some clothes. Over the years, I had sent most of my papers, magazines, and books to my mother for safekeeping.

My last day in prison should have been one of joy, but as in the past, I was overwhelmed; everything felt dreamlike. I worried about my relationship with Mercedes. She had grown up while I was in prison. How could I reconnect with a sixteen-year-old stranger? I would have to get to know her first. I also recognized the influence that my parents had on her. They had baptized her as a Jehovah's Witness. At that point, she was their daughter, not mine. Her beliefs and thoughts belonged to a world I had rejected years ago. My mother believed the world would end soon. I thought it was just beginning.

I walked to the front gate. A guard said, "See you later!"

"No, you won't," I replied.

The guard laughed.

My sister Net and her husband met me at the gate shortly after 9:00 A.M. We hugged for a long time. I climbed into the back seat of their car and headed to Chicago. Net called our mother. "We got her," she said. They drove around the city, showing me how things had changed. The Chicago Housing Authority had demolished the Lake Michigan High-Rises and most other high-rises the year before, amid concerns that the city's public housing had been a social engineering mistake — a "no-man's-land" of broken windows, stabbings, and drug deals.

In their place stood rows of new three-story buildings. The sidewalks were clean and lined with newly planted trees. Everything looked so different. I felt disoriented. Everything I knew was gone.

Net's relationship with our mother had changed, too. For a while, Net had read the *Watchtower* magazines and studied the Bible with our mother. While she was "studying," as the Witnesses call it, Mama visited her all the time. Then Net changed her mind. She told Mama she wouldn't become a Witness, and she didn't want to "study" anymore. Mama never set foot in her house again.

We drove to Mama and Daddy's place, a first-floor apartment in a two-story building on South Green Street on the South Side of Chicago.

I hugged my parents. My father wiped his eyes. Everything seemed surreal. Mercedes was in her room, asleep. I opened her bedroom door, walked to her bed, and whispered her name. She woke up with a start and reached out for me. When she was a baby, she would reach out for me the same way, waiting for me to pick her up from her crib. We hugged for a long time. Neither of us cried.

We didn't talk about prison. When Mercedes was in elementary school, my parents told her that James and I had gotten into a fight, and he had gotten hurt and had died.

"That's why it's not good for people to fight," they said.

Friends and relatives stopped by. We laughed and hugged. As I walked around the apartment, my daughter watched me. "I feel like I'm in a dream," she said.

I did, too.

My parents had only two bedrooms. For the first few days, I slept in the twin-size bed with Mercedes, holding her as she slept. After that, I moved to the couch. We were both okay with that.

After a few days, I asked my mother where she kept my things. I had mailed her all my prison letters, newspaper editorials, and books, including copies of the Bhagavad Gita and the Qur'an. I had so much paper that prison officials deemed my cell a fire hazard. I wanted to revisit everything now that I was out; I needed them to help get my bearings.

Almost everything was gone.

"You don't need any of that," my mother said. "It's not the truth."

Magazines with my byline, newspaper op-eds, newsletters with addresses, letters from friends — my mother had thrown them into the trash, even though she could store things in a detached garage.

"I couldn't keep everything in the garage. It was a fire hazard," my mother explained.

I blinked. She sounded like a prison guard. She never warned me that she couldn't store my stuff. She never gave me a chance to find another place for my possessions. She combed through fourteen years of my life and picked out what she thought I "needed." I was stunned. But I had learned as a child that it was futile to protest.

"It's done now," she said, using the same tone she had always used when dismissing my concerns. "It's done now," she repeated.

I was home.

Even though I was a felon, I was sure I could get a job. I turned to the Safer Foundation for help. The Chicago-based organization helped ex-prisoners find work and become "law-abiding members of the community." I thought it would be easy for them to place me somewhere. I had earned degrees in applied science, commercial arts and photography, and computer technology in prison. I had a paralegal certificate. And I had worked as a secretary in Chicago before my arrest.

I typed my résumé on my parents' home computer and printed it out. On the morning of my appointment, I dressed in black slacks and a pink sweater. I rode the bus downtown and filled out paperwork at the front desk. When one of the women who worked there called my name, I confidently approached her desk.

"We can't help you," she said. "Your release papers say that you need mental health counseling before we can work with you."

I stared at her for what seemed like a full minute. I had spent fourteen years in the Illinois Department of Corrections. No one had ever suggested I get psychological counseling.

"If the prison officials at Dwight felt I needed therapy, why didn't they give it to me during the fourteen years I was there?" I asked.

"I don't know," she said. "I'm sorry."

She gave me a list of places where I could go through formal counseling and told me to come back after I had completed the program.

I took the bus back to my parents' house, stunned.

When I got home, I looked at the list she had given me and realized one of the places was just a couple of blocks away. I picked up my shattered expectations of coming home with a job and walked to the counseling agency near South Green Street.

A woman at the front desk asked me for my address.

"You're not in our territory," she said. "We can't help you."

I pointed out that I lived two blocks away and had just walked to their office.

"Our territory doesn't include our office location or where you live," she said. "You need to talk to someone on the West Side of Chicago." She gave me an address. The agency was more than an hour away.

"How can I pay the bus fare without a job?" I asked.

"I don't know," she said. "I'm sorry."

I walked back home and told my mother what had happened. She said she would drive me to the location they gave me. I signed in at the front desk and waited forty-five minutes to be called into an office.

Finally, a woman called me into a back office. She looked through a folder — I'm not sure where it came from — and then said I would need to spend three days a week in counseling at their office.

I asked her the same questions I'd asked the others. Why didn't Dwight or Dixon Correctional Center provide mental health counseling while I was in their custody for fourteen years? Why would they block me from getting work? Why couldn't I go to the mental health clinic two blocks from my home instead of taking a bus across town? How could I afford the bus fare to their office and back home three days a week if I couldn't work? And how was I supposed to support myself in the meantime if I couldn't work and get counseling at the same time?

"I can see why you've been referred to us," the woman said snidely, with a sneer on her face. "It's obvious that you're angry and hostile."

I walked back to the waiting area and told my mother what happened.

"I see why people get out and go right back to prison!" my mother exploded. "They act like they *want* you to go back!"

PRISON ACTION COMMITTEE

I got around the counseling requirement by calling James P. Chapman, an attorney I'd met in prison. My timing was perfect. Chapman had made a name for himself working with prisoners. In 1991, he met with six prisoners at the Stateville Correctional Center, a maximum-security prison in Joliet, Illinois. The six men — Black, Latino, and white — had developed ideas for prison reform and programs to help ex-cons stay out of jail. But no one would listen to them. Chapman agreed to set up an organization that would serve as a voice for prisoners. It would be staffed exclusively by men and women who had been imprisoned in the Illinois Department of Corrections and had demonstrated a positive attitude while behind bars. The board of directors would include people still in prison — ideal commentators on prison policies and conditions.

In 1992, ex-prisoner Richard Baker became the first executive director of the Prison Action Committee, or PAC. The agency operated out of two small rooms in Jim Chapman's downtown Chicago law office. Six years later, Chapman founded the Illinois Institute for Community Law and Affairs to concentrate on recidivism and serve as PAC's educational and legal arm.

By the time I was released in 1999, PAC had a full-time staff of four former prisoners working out of a separate office on Chicago's South Side. There was also a learning center on the Northwest Side. It seemed like a good organization, one that could improve prison conditions and help ex-cons get jobs and stay out of jail.

But the institute's executive director had recently left the position after a falling-out with Jim Chapman, so Jim asked me to become the new executive director and project manager. The job only paid $250 a week, but I believed in the institute's mission. And I needed the work. In January 2000, after I had been home for less than a month, I landed a job with an impressive title. I was no longer inmate N77122.

I rode the 79th Street bus to work. The office included six desks with computers and a bathroom in the back. Chapman had hired someone to clean the office once a week. Five of the desks were for people — all former prisoners — who worked for PAC. I was the only person who worked for the institute. On most days, I was the first one in the office.

After a couple of weeks, I came home from work and was sitting at the kitchen table when my father walked out of the bedroom. "How's the search for an apartment coming along?" he asked me.

I stared at him. I hadn't started looking for an apartment. I had only been home for about six weeks, and in my below-minimum-wage job for about two weeks. I had envisioned staying with my parents until I was able to get on my feet.

Then my mother came into the kitchen and said the landlord had said something about me living there. He had called me "a *murderer!*" she said.

"You need to hurry up and find an apartment," my mother said.

I turned to a friend for help, Imam Abdul Alim Bashir, the Muslim chaplain at Dwight. When I'd been in isolation, Bashir had visited me once a week. After about six months, he said he wanted to marry me. He was in his sixties, with gray hair and missing teeth. He carried an overstuffed briefcase, wore a multicolored caftan under his suit, and had once been a part of the Nation of Islam under Elijah Muhammad. In fact, he had been one of Malcolm X's bodyguards. He even owned a tape recorder Malcolm used to record speeches.

After rejoining the prison population, I attended his weekly prison services. He gave me his home phone number, and I called him a few times a week.

One day he told me he had met someone else and they were going to be married. He had grown lonely waiting for me to get out but said, "You can continue to call me and let me know how you're doing."

I was devastated. This was the second time a man had proposed to me and then changed his mind. I did not call him again.

I had given him my parents' phone number so he could meet my daughter. That didn't happen, but Bashir continued to stay in touch with my parents, even after I stopped talking to him. When I came home, I called to let him know that I was home and learned his third marriage had fallen apart.

Bashir helped me find an apartment in a three-story brick building near the tree-lined intersection of 78th and Ridgeland Avenue. Bashir and Jim Chapman knew each other from their work with the Illinois Department of Corrections. Jim gave me the money for the security deposit and the first month's rent. It was a rough place. People screamed and cursed all night long in the newly renovated building. Others stood on the corner beneath my second-floor window and sold drugs.

I was working for Jim, but Bashir regularly visited me at the office. Sometimes he would stay all day and chat. Other times, we would go to lunch together. His frequent visits upset Jim, who huffed, "Every time this *old man* comes by, you can't just jump up and leave the office!"

Every Tuesday, I worked with Jim at the institute's free legal clinic in the back of a small Baptist church, one of the hundreds of Black churches on Chicago's South Side. The clinic wasn't just for former prisoners. Anybody could come — and they did.

"What brings you to the clinic?" I asked each of them. I tried to make each person feel they were talking to someone who cared. Because I did.

I recorded their problems: filthy, unsafe housing, apartments with no heat, workplace discrimination. I asked people for their names, addresses, telephone numbers, job locations, and Social Security numbers, and I told them that Jim Chapman, an attorney, would be in touch.

The work inspired me. I felt like we could make a difference. These people needed more than Band-Aid solutions and a pep talk. They needed an exit ramp off the "same problem, different day" life that wore them down.

I needed that exit ramp, too. I thought I could find it by helping others.

Every Friday, Jim called me for a *detailed* report. After a few months, I discovered that Jim rarely scheduled a second meeting with the people seeking help. I began to feel uneasy. *Are we helping anyone?* I wondered. One day, when he asked me for my report, I confronted him.

"Have you followed up with anyone from my previous reports?" I asked.

"It's not your job to question what I'm doing," he growled. "Your job is to provide me with information. Just make sure you send a report every week."

One day I spoke to Carlos Vega, one of PAC's founders, and he revealed that the prisoners inside Stateville Correctional Center had intended for PAC to be a vigilante organization. Prison guards who beat prisoners were rarely punished, so the prisoners decided to organize a group of men who, upon their release, would punish guards who had beaten or killed prisoners.

"There are already plenty of organizations with GED programs!" Carlos exploded. "That's not what PAC was supposed to be!"

According to Carlos, the "brothers" who promised to retaliate against brutal guards did nothing once they got out of prison. They all said they didn't want to get into trouble, and as a result, PAC became just another nonprofit organization helping ex-cons get diplomas.

Carlos had other complaints, too. Jim Chapman had seized control of the agency, he said. Meanwhile, PAC focused on chasing grant money, which enabled the agency to dole out low-paying jobs to former prisoners. One of the four full-time employees, an African American man, lived in a homeless shelter while employed at PAC. Working at PAC had become a trap, but the former prisoners who worked there felt lucky just to have a job.

"*None* of us could make it out there in the real world," Carlos said. "*None* of us!"

It was an eye-opening perspective. I didn't realize that the people I worked with every day felt that way about themselves — and about me. I started calling people without Jim's knowledge. I asked them if they still needed assistance. Increasingly, people did not want to speak with me. "No, thank you, I don't need any help," they said and hung up the phone. I wondered, had they heard that something was not right at the institute or with Jim?

Their responses upset me. I was trying to help people in the community. I thought I might become a community organizer one day. The last thing I needed was a bad reputation with the people who lived in the community.

It didn't help that Jim asked me to dinner at least once a week. I wondered what his real motivation was for keeping me around him for what seemed to me like almost all the time. I barely had time or energy to do anything else with anybody else. I was working twelve or more hours a day and making very little money. If you divided my paycheck by the number of hours I worked, I earned less than minimum wage. Every night I came home exhausted. Would the institute ever follow up on my reports? Jim told me not to worry about it.

I couldn't accept that. I wanted to know what was going on.

When I pressed him, he fired me.

"Don't worry about it," Bashir told me. He seemed glad.

LEGACY THEATRE

The next week, Bashir called Rasheed Akbar, a former prisoner and theater owner. He had been a counselor with the PACE program in the Cook County Jail while I was there. PACE, or Programmed Activities for Correctional Education, is a school located within the Cook County Jail into which detainees can voluntarily enroll upon entry with the goal of earning their GED. Ironically, PACE operated under the Safer Foundation — the same organization that wouldn't help me find employment when I got out.

Rasheed owned the Legacy Theatre, a Black-themed live theater in Blue Island, Illinois. Located at 12952 Western Avenue, the venue was somewhat out of place in that the surrounding neighborhood was home primarily to Hispanics and whites. The theater put on great live shows, but attendance was embarrassingly poor. The actors, most of them talented professionals, deserved better.

Rasheed needed a secretary to help him run the theater, which was failing spectacularly. Even the telephone service had been cut off. I wanted to help, and I needed a job. I got up early and took a long bus ride from the inner city to the suburbs. Because most of the shows ran on the weekend, I often worked seven days a week.

I assumed that I would get paid every two weeks — even though Rasheed had never given me any onboarding paperwork. *Maybe he's going to pay me in cash*, I thought. At the end of the first two weeks, I asked him about my paycheck.

"The theater is running a little short right now," he said. "If you can hang in there with me, I'll get your pay caught up."

Since I had a couple more weeks until my next rent payment was due, I thought that would work.

"I need something to carry me through, though," I told him. "It costs me bus fare just to get here, and I have to buy food."

He reached in his pocket and gave me a hundred dollars.

Two weeks later, and with my rent now due, I asked him again about my paycheck.

"I'll take care of it," he said, as he hurriedly walked by me.

At that point I realized that Rasheed never intended to pay me. He didn't even have a payroll system. Later, I discovered that Rasheed routinely stiffed employees. He would string them along with promises, and when they quit, he hired someone new. Once again, I felt betrayed. Rasheed knew I had just gotten out of prison and needed rent and food money. Once more, I turned to Bashir. He gave me the money to pay my rent and said he would talk to Rasheed.

After that, Bashir stayed at my apartment whenever he felt like it. It felt natural to me. After all, when Chapman fired me, Bashir helped me find another job. And when Rasheed refused to pay me, Bashir gave me money. When he confronted Rasheed, Rasheed finally paid me what he owed me.

I didn't think of Bashir romantically, but I thought he was in my corner. I felt like he would defend me and challenge anyone who mistreated me. I had never felt like anyone was on my side until he came along.

During this time, I visited a naturopath. She told me herbs would cleanse my body of the toxins I had accumulated from eating bad prison food for fourteen years. That made sense to me. She gave me a concoction to drink twice a day. After the second day, it burned me from the inside out. I looked like a burn victim; my skin wept fluid constantly. I couldn't sleep because my back was raw, and my skin hurt everywhere. I wasn't menopausal, but I began to suffer from intense hot flashes. Reptilian-like scales formed on my face and neck. I had never been so sick or ugly in my life. A doctor prescribed the steroid prednisone, which cleared up my skin but made me gain weight.

Again, Bashir came to my aid. He brought me food and took me out despite my appearance. I was grateful for the attention, but it made me feel indebted to him.

I didn't want to marry Bashir, not at first. I didn't love him. Instead, I thought of him as a friend. But when I expressed my feelings to my mother and my oldest sister, they were dismissive. Bashir will make a good husband, they said. My mother was impressed by how good a friend Bashir had been to me. Bashir had recently retired. A monthly Social Security check and his state pension allowed him to live comfortably.

Nine months after I got home from prison, I agreed with my mother and sister. Bashir must really love me because he stood by me when I was sick, broke, and scary looking. So I agreed to marry Bashir — a man who had been divorced three times and was three months younger than my father.

MY DAY

Once we became engaged, Bashir grew much more controlling. On Sunday mornings, he had Islamic studies with a group of scholars who pressed him to follow Muslim customs for our upcoming wedding. The men and women should be kept separate, they said, and Bashir insisted we accommodate their wishes. One day, when he was telling me yet again how his friends and scholars thought we should plan our wedding, I said, "Bashir, the wedding day is supposed to be about the *bride*! This is supposed to be *my* day! It's not supposed to be about what your friends want!"

Bashir stared at me. He said that his friends had a lot of money, but if they didn't approve of the ceremony, they wouldn't attend and they wouldn't give us a wedding present.

I didn't care about their presents. I wanted to plan my wedding.

Bashir drove me everywhere. When I shopped for my wedding dress, he tagged along. "Since I'm paying for it, I want to make sure I like it," he said. I found a silver evening gown at Bergner's in a mall in Champaign, Illinois. A friend of Bashir's — a woman who was part of the Nation of Islam and who had befriended me as well — loaned me a beautiful silver scarf to cover my head.

Another friend of Bashir's owned a strip mall furniture store with a large meeting hall attached to it. Bashir asked him if we could get married there, and he said he would be honored to host our wedding and reception. I decorated the room with silver and white balloons from Party City. I placed red roses and silver candlesticks with white candles on long folding tables draped with white tablecloths.

My mother called and said my father wouldn't be able to walk me down the aisle because Bashir was a Muslim. I didn't try to change his mind. I didn't even ask to speak to him. I did wonder, though, why my mother was speaking for him. Why couldn't he tell me that himself?

I'll walk down the aisle by myself, I thought.

My daughter spent the night before the wedding with me. She was happy for me, but she didn't like Bashir. She thought he was rude. He was always talking about people's weight. She wasn't pleased about my moving to Pontiac, Illinois, where Bashir worked in the local prison. Bashir's apartment was an hour and a half from Chicago, and I assured Mercedes she could visit me anytime.

Because I did not have a car or a driver's license, I asked my sister Faye to drive Mercedes and me to the wedding hall. We set a time for her to pick me up, but on the day of my wedding, Faye was a no-show. She didn't even call. I called Bashir and told him I needed a ride. Bashir came and picked me up, and the groom drove the bride to the wedding. It wasn't even remotely how I had envisioned my wedding day.

My parents attended as guests rather than as the parents of the bride. They sat in the audience with my landlord, whom I had also invited. My mother didn't help me with my wedding dress, my decorations, or any last-minute details. Only one of my siblings, my oldest brother, Townsell, showed up. At the last minute, I asked him to walk me down the aisle, and he did.

Bashir's friends stayed away. They sent no wedding presents.

When I spoke to my sister Faye a few weeks later, I asked her why she didn't drive me to my wedding. She said, "I forgot!" and laughed.

"You didn't forget," I said. "Mama told me you called her after the wedding and asked her how it had gone."

Faye said nothing.

My oldest sister, Net, stayed away, too. After I left prison, I spent a lot of time with her and her husband. I thought we were getting close. She had even encouraged me to marry Bashir.

"I don't *feel* anything when I'm with him," I had protested.

"Girl, that don't matter," Net had said.

Our mother agreed. "Bashir is crazy about you," she said. "He told me he wants to take you around the world."

But as soon as I got engaged, Net stopped speaking to me. She stopped answering the telephone when I called her.

All but one of Bashir's daughters stayed away. Later, I found out why. Bashir's birthday was October 12 — just a few weeks after the wedding. His daughters had been planning a surprise birthday party for him in Atlanta. I did not know about the party because none of his daughters made me a part of the family's plans.

Bashir and I sent wedding invitations to several of his friends in Cincinnati, his old stomping grounds. They had assured us they would attend. Then they got the surprise birthday party notice and most were unable to attend both.

When they called Bashir's daughters and told them that they had already committed to the wedding, they convinced everybody to choose the birthday party instead. No one told me they couldn't make it. I ordered enough food from the caterer to feed all the people who had RSVP'd yes. The caterer was a longtime friend of Bashir. He cooked chicken, rice, and a variety of well-seasoned and tender vegetables. He offered a variety of non-alcoholic drinks, too. And his Swedish meatballs won over everybody. Our wedding cake was vanilla with cream cheese frosting. Everything was delicious, but we paid for twice the food we needed. Everybody took multiple plates home.

I felt like I had completed a long journey and was about to start a new chapter in my life. I wanted to dance at my wedding to a song that expressed those sentiments, and I chose "The Long and Winding Road," a Beatles song covered by Billy Ocean. I found it on cassette tape and planned to surprise the deejay with it — my special request.

Suddenly, Bashir stood up, got everyone's attention, and said he had an announcement.

"There will be no dancing at our wedding," he said.

I sat at the head table, stunned.

I married Bashir on September 24, 2000. In prison, I had called him by his title, Imam Bashir. After we got married, I called him Bashir. I never called him by his first name.

book two

Atlanta

NEW CAR, NEW HOME, NEW LIFE

Ironically, my marriage thrust me back into prison life. We lived in Bashir's apartment in Pontiac, a small prison town where practically everyone, including my husband, had connections to Pontiac Correctional Center. Bashir served as the Muslim chaplain, and we could walk to the prison from our apartment. At the local grocery stores, I sometimes ran into former guards from Dwight Correctional Center.

Luckily, Bashir wanted to be closer to his daughters in Atlanta. So, in 2001, we started looking at houses in the area. The idea of being a homeowner mesmerized me. I didn't stop to think about what the move would mean to my daughter. I had spent fourteen years apart from her, and I was still getting to know her. We had grown closer, but a breach still existed. She was a full-fledged Jehovah's Witness: She worshipped at the Kingdom Hall, handed out *Awake!*, and had other Jehovah's Witnesses as friends.

The drive south unsettled me. At some point, the trees began to look like people. I saw blurry afterimages along the highway. Were they the ghosts of the people who had been lynched?

We found a house in a new subdivision called Hidden Creek in Loganville, forty miles from Atlanta. We wrote a rubber check as earnest money and headed home. On the drive home, we brainstormed ways to come up with the down payment. I was behind the wheel of our Honda Accord. I had been driving for only a couple of years, and I had never learned how to merge. I tried to merge onto the highway just as a truck passed by. Suddenly I was driving on the shoulder alongside the truck. At first, I didn't know I was on the shoulder. When I realized that I hadn't merged onto the highway, I panicked. It didn't occur to me that I could have stopped. For some reason, I thought that if I stopped, someone would hit me from behind. I hit the accelerator and tried to get in front of the truck. I almost made it, but the truck clipped the Honda's left taillight. We went spinning in circles across a four-lane highway and down the embankment. Mercifully, we didn't collide with any other cars or trucks.

A highway patrolman cited both of us. I should have never mistaken the shoulder for the road, he said. But the truck driver should have seen that I was in trouble and slowed down, he added.

A lot of people stopped and offered to help. Some of them seemed surprised we were alive, let alone uninjured. Equally surprising: The truck left only a small dent in the Honda. We were towed to a garage, where mechanics popped the tires back on the car and filled them with air. Bashir took the wheel after that.

When our insurance agent looked at the damage to the car, he said the company would write a check for the damage. It was exactly what we needed for a down payment on our new house. We cashed the check. We never repaired the dent.

Just before we moved, I said good-bye to my parents and Mercedes. My daughter said, "Every time you move somewhere, it's farther and farther away from me."

I invited her to stay with me, and I showed her pictures of the house. It had three bedrooms, two bathrooms, an upstairs office, a big open kitchen, and a big green yard. The photographs won her over.

"You'll have a new place to visit. And you can stay as long as you want," I said.

But it was a long drive: more than eleven hours. The reality was, I couldn't build my life around a desire to raise my daughter. That time had come and gone. My focus had to be on creating a life for myself that I could be proud of — a life that Mercedes would want to be a part of.

We closed on the house, moved, and drove the Honda for a few more months before buying a new one, a silver Special Edition. It was the first new car Bashir had owned. He loved it.

While I was in Georgia, Mercedes went to Chicago City Hall and married a young man who was also a Jehovah's Witness. When they came to Loganville to visit us, we gave them our old car and they drove back to Chicago in it.

I felt proud I had been able to give my daughter something significant.

FREE

In Illinois, following my release from prison, I had a certain amount of freedom, even though I was on parole for three years. When I lived in Chicago, I went to a parole office front desk and signed a card stating that I was staying clean — no drugs — and looking for work. In Pontiac, a short white woman with a friendly manner came to Bashir's apartment and helped me get a transfer out of state when we decided to move to Georgia. But once I left the state where I had been convicted, I had to wear an ankle monitor.

Once a month Bashir drove me to the parole office in Monroe, a rural spot an hour from Atlanta. Monroe was a part of the old South. Its mills had once spun cotton, and it was the site of the last mass lynching in America. In July 1946, a white mob attacked and killed two Black married couples who drove through the area.

My new parole officer, a large, burly man, fastened a monitor on my left ankle so a GPS device could track my movements. Someone was always monitoring me. If I left my house, they would know it, in effect turning my home into a well-decorated prison.

"You can't go farther than 150 feet from your house," the parole officer said.

"That's a problem," I said. "My house sits on nearly three-quarters of an acre of land. My backyard is more than 150 feet from the inside of my house."

He agreed to extend the range so I could walk in the yard.

I could leave home to go to the local grocery store and some other permitted outings, but I had to call before leaving, I had to keep receipts to prove where I had been, and I could not be out after 7:00 P.M.

I asked the officer to fasten the monitor on my left ankle — the ankle I broke during my attempted prison escape, which was much skinnier than my right leg — because I thought it would hide my large keloid scars.

The strategy backfired. The old injuries filled with fluid and wept beneath the metal and plastic monitor. I developed a new rash on top of the old marks. Still, I knew better than to try to remove the monitor. Tampering with an ankle monitor is a felony, and I was not going back to prison. I wore it everywhere, even in the shower. But I did try to hide it. I wore jeans, or slacks, or very long dresses, which my Muslim husband preferred, anyway. But it was always there.

Because I had a curfew, I couldn't go to social events or dine with my husband's friends or family. My husband explained to people why I couldn't join them. I pretended not to be embarrassed, but I was. I felt isolated and excluded.

On June 13, 2002, I went to see my parole officer. He handed me a piece of paper, Form 3-48. "This discharge allows you to vote, run for public office and sit on a jury," it said. "It DOES NOT restore your right to carry a firearm."

I couldn't wait to sign it.

The officer made a copy of the signed form and gave me the original. He then deactivated the ankle monitor with its GPS device, removed the metal band from around my ankle, and wished me luck.

When I looked at my leg, I wanted to cry — partly out of joy, partly out of relief, and partly because the skin on my ankle looked rotten.

"Thank Allah that's over," my husband said.

I wanted to celebrate and stay out late. Bashir wanted to go home, sit on the couch, and watch CNN. He did nothing special for me that day. Even so, for the first time in years, I felt like I could finally live a normal life. We made plans to visit his friends in Miami and

Cincinnati. I went to the mosque. I no longer had to save my grocery receipts.

On January 1, 2003, the Illinois Department of Corrections officially freed me for good. The Field Services Office of the Dixon Correctional Center confirmed I had completed my sentence. "On this date, your obligation to the department ceases," the state said. "We take this opportunity to congratulate you on the successful completion of your supervision and wish you continued success."

If I could have turned a somersault, I would have. I had been on parole for three years, starting in Illinois and finishing up in Georgia.

Now the leash was off.

I was ready to reinvent myself.

In search of a new identity, I tested my maternal DNA through African Ancestry. I scraped the insides of both cheeks with a swab, mailed the samples to the agency, and waited. The results surprised me. On my mother's side, I had genetic markers that matched the Temne people in the West African country of Sierra Leone. I went online and started learning about my ancestral home.

Amazingly, I lived twenty minutes from the president of an organization called the Friends of Sierra Leone, which included many former Peace Corps volunteers who had worked in Sierra Leone. I also discovered that the pharmacist at the local Walmart was from Sierra Leone. We struck up a friendship, and he invited me to a few social events. The people were warm and friendly. Eventually, the organization asked me to serve on their board, and for two years I chaired the membership committee.

I emailed Joseph Opala, a former Peace Corps volunteer who taught at James Madison University in Virginia. Opala had spent seventeen years in Sierra Leone as a teacher, researcher, and government consultant before the rebel war forced him to flee the country in a crowded fishing boat in 1991. I introduced myself and said I had just traced my maternal DNA back to Sierra Leone and I was interested in what he knew about the country and its history. Through Opala, I learned that an old slave fort in the Sierra Leone River was one of the most lucrative slave trading operations in West Africa. Founded about 1670, the Bunce Island slave fort exported tens of thousands of African captives to North America and the West Indies until the British Parliament closed it down in 1808. The fort had collapsed in spots, and the original wood was gone, but Opala hoped to restore the eighteenth-century fort through advanced computer graphics. The idea of re-creating a slave castle through 3-D animation fascinated me.

I connected to the larger world in other ways. In Illinois, I had worked for agencies created to help ex-prisoners. In Georgia, I did the same. For the next seven years, I worked with individuals in the African American Muslim community who wanted to help those who had run afoul of the law. I met most of them at the Masjid of Al-Islam for Jumah mosque, where Bashir prayed on Fridays. Many of the members were older Black Christians who had converted to Islam. A lot of people, some of them former prisoners, were frustrated with organizations that claimed to help ex-cons but didn't. A few of them had started or wanted to start new and better nonprofits — "ones that worked." But most of those proposed organizations failed to launch. They needed grant money to get started and grant money to keep going. In the end, if they managed to stay afloat, they operated no differently from the already existing nonprofits they complained about.

It was a familiar story. They duplicated each other's efforts in providing GED instruction and vocational training. They tried but mostly failed to help former prisoners find housing. They spent most of their time writing grant proposals, exaggerating their successes, and scrambling to keep the lights on and the doors open. No one could escape the grant money treadmill. If organizers wanted state or federal money, they had to write proposals for programs that were likely to get funded — the same old GED and job training programs that everybody else already offered.

Meanwhile, the recidivism problem was getting worse. Ex-cons kept going back to jail. Georgia boasted the fifth-largest prison system in the nation. The state spent $1 billion a year to run it.

Even Newt Gingrich, the former Republican congressman and Speaker of the House, later admitted the system had failed. Recidivism rates were unacceptably high, he told *The Atlanta Journal-Constitution*. Churches and nonprofits had to do more to help ex-cons lead productive lives.

I agreed. America's ex-cons, myself included, needed help.

ENTREPRENEUR

After moving to Georgia, I continued to work temp jobs throughout the Atlanta area until I landed a full-time job as a title processor for First Title Corporation in Duluth, Georgia. I worked there for two years, from 2002 through 2004 — including during the time that I wore the ankle monitor. I made sure no one ever saw it. Working there reminded me of working at Lloyd's of London. And it was just as dull.

Eventually the company downsized. I was among those who were laid off.

I collected unemployment for several months before I got a job at Wagner, Johnston & Rosenthal, a law firm in Sandy Springs. I had a paralegal certificate, but I worked as a receptionist. Sometimes I did legal work when the legal secretaries needed help. They paid me $28,000 per year.

"I don't know anybody who works even as a receptionist who makes less than $30,000 a year," the office manager had told me.

But I never tried to go back and renegotiate my salary. I had fallen into the trap of just being "glad to have a job." I wasn't thinking about what my work was worth.

Monday through Friday, I steered our silver Honda Accord onto I-285, known locally as the Perimeter — one of the most dangerous interstates in America. It was notorious for its daily dose of deadly crashes — particularly between cars and semi-trucks. Lots of people who lived in Atlanta avoided driving on it. But it was the most direct route from my house to my job. I gritted my teeth and made the rush-hour trip twice a day.

Despite the white-knuckled commute for ridiculously low pay, I kept the job because I needed the money to start my own business. I enrolled in DeVry University, which offered a degree in business administration focusing on small business management and entrepreneurship.

I wanted to develop a process to use familiar foods in new ways based on a concept I thought could turn legumes and vegetables into healthy snacks and desserts. In addition to business classes, I studied statistics, financial accounting, management principles, marketing, project management, and managerial accounting.

I studied at work, drove home, and studied at night.

Bashir watched television and ignored me, but I didn't care; I felt productive. I took all of my classes online. After graduation, I spent my free time and money on creating my food business. I contacted a company in New York called Capico International, which I had found through an internet search. Ron Hari said his company could help me develop, market, and sell proprietary food products to customers worldwide. He said he had decades of experience in successfully launching entrepreneurial food companies and gave me references, which I called. Bashir and I even met Hari in New York, where he took us on a tour of the plant where he said my foods would be made and packaged.

I signed a contract for Ron to help me develop my product and distribute it through Restaurant Depot. He said he had done this before for other food entrepreneurs. I paid him $6,000, and he did nothing. In an email, he told me he had been diagnosed with cancer. He said he would start work on our project when he felt better. I badgered him via email for a year and a half. If you're unable to proceed, you should return my money, I said. He promised he would get back to work soon. I realized he had tricked me and stolen my money, but I didn't have the money to hire an attorney.

I pressed on. I was as doggedly determined to make a success of my food business as I was to make a success of my marriage. No matter how bad it was going, I didn't want to fail at it. I didn't know when to cut my losses. I began working with the Food Entrepreneur Assistance Program at the University of Nebraska–Lincoln to develop my product, transforming it from a recipe into a commercial formula. The program turned out to be a good fit. The manager and the food scientists, professional and easy to work with, assisted me in refining my ideas. But by then, I could no longer concentrate on my business. I was headed to divorce court.

MARRYING MOMMY

I had a new house and a new car parked in my two-car garage. I had been able to do something to help my daughter and her new husband. I had planted fruit trees and rosebushes and started gardening and cooking. I had landed several jobs despite my felony background. I should have been on top of the world. Instead, I was lonely and miserable. I retreated to the bedroom, where I lived in a world of books — just as I had done as a child and as a prisoner.

I had spent fourteen years behind bars, isolated and alone among hundreds of inmates. Nine months after my release I was married — and back in solitary confinement. All I did was work, come home, and take care of Bashir. I had no social life, no friends; I rarely spoke to anyone. Whenever I went anywhere — including to the grocery store — Bashir came, too. If I engaged anyone in conversation, especially a man, he blew his top. Of course, he talked to anyone he wanted to, male or female.

My life was less free and less interesting than when I lived behind bars. The prison guards had been more respectful and interested in my ideas than my husband. They asked me about the books I was reading. They kidded me, too, because I was a New York Knicks fan in a prison full of Chicago Bulls fans *during* the Michael Jordan–Phil Jackson era of multiple NBA championships.

The Knicks: Patrick Ewing, John Starks, Charles Oakley, Anthony Mason, Greg Anthony, Doug Christie, even the coach, Pat Riley — their style matched my own. They did not play a pretty game. They played an unapologetically physical game. I genuinely loved watching them, and I understood the game. When the Knicks and the Bulls played each other, the inmates watched the games in the dayroom. The officers and some of the inmates got a kick out of my rooting for the Knicks. There was a lot of friendly teasing.

When I cleaned the dayroom after lockup (which was my work assignment at one point — "housegirl"), certain guards would talk to me about the news. They knew I was well read. One day I sat in the dayroom reading *The Fall of America* by Elijah Muhammad. One of the guards said, "So what if America falls? Look at history. Every civilization has fallen. Look at Rome." The guard had a reputation for being racist, but he talked to me, and I enjoyed our conversations. We shared our opinions on recent events, local politics, even race. Many of the guards had views that differed from mine, but it didn't matter to me. I was starved for talk that didn't revolve around prison life.

One day I told Bashir he had taken advantage of me. He had seen me at a point when I was needy and vulnerable. My parents had pressured me to move. I never got a chance to get out, explore life, or find my bearings before I married a man thirty-six years my senior. He had swooped in under the guise of helping me, but really, he did it for himself. Our marriage provided him with a young wife who could sacrifice her future for him, a woman who could cook, clean, and be his full-time caregiver. It was a great deal for him. When I told him that, he simply stared at me. But he didn't deny it.

I began to connect my marriage to my past. People say that men marry their mothers, and women marry their fathers, but my life wasn't that simple.

I had married a man who was my father's age but who had my mother's icy, distant, disapproving, and overbearing demeanor — a combination of my parents. On the other hand, my husband was exactly like my father in one way: He loved to talk. He told complete strangers all our personal business. He craved attention and approval. Similarly, if I spoke to Bashir privately, he immediately called his daughters and told them everything, no matter how mundane the subject.

"I just want y'all to know what we're talking about," he would say.

One weekend morning, an hour or so after lying in bed and sharing certain thoughts with Bashir, the kinds of things married couples discuss, I went outside to see what he was up to. He stood on the front lawn talking to a neighbor, telling her everything I had said in bed.

Not only had I married a composite of my parents, I had also married into a family much like my own, where I enjoyed no privacy and received little respect or attention.

When Bashir and I bought our new house, his daughters had claimed he had moved too far away for them to visit regularly. So I knew they were in the general vicinity, but I thought they were far enough away for Bashir and I to build our own life together without interference. I discovered only after we had moved into it that the house was less than twenty minutes from where Bashir's first wife lived with their five adult daughters.

One year, Bashir's daughters planned a family reunion in Atlanta. Relatives from around the country were coming. There was one problem, however. They decided to hold the reunion at our house without asking us. They simply sent invitations to everyone in the family, listing our address for the event. They never discussed the plan with us. In fact, they didn't even show us the invitation. Bashir discovered their plan while speaking on the telephone to one of his nephews in New York.

"I'll see you next month at the family reunion!" Bashir's nephew announced.

"Oh yeah?" Bashir said.

"Yeah, I'm coming! I'm looking forward to seeing your house!"

"Oh, I don't know anything about that," Bashir said. "You sure it's at my house?"

"Yeah!" his nephew said. "You'd better talk to your daughters!"

Bashir did. "What's this about a family reunion?" he asked Nadiyah. "It's supposed to be at my house?"

"Oh yeah," she said. "I thought you knew."

I pitched a fit.

"How can your daughters possibly think it's appropriate to plan a family reunion at our home and not say one word to me about it?"

Just like my mother, Bashir blamed me.

"Maybe it's your fault," he said. "Maybe they don't feel like they can really relate to you."

The realization hit me like a thunderbolt: I was reliving my childhood.

I had become part of an extended family in which I was once again, in effect, the youngest of six children. Since Bashir did not treat me like a mate and an equal, I was essentially relegated to being a child — and, once again, the least important one. And just as my siblings had done growing up in Chicago, my husband's daughters ignored me on the one hand, while complaining about and competing with me on the other.

Through my marriage, I had re-created my childhood. The parallel was so striking that it cut through the fog of my despair. For the first time, I saw that I was stuck in a loop — having the same relationships with different people, living the same life in different houses. While I did not know at the time that the "loop" experience is common to those suffering from post-traumatic stress disorder, it was the first time that I could see my problem. I had to break out of the loop.

My marriage had degenerated into a battlefield. If I said yes, Bashir said no. If I wanted him to do something, not doing it became his sole mission in life. If I asked him not to do something, nothing in the world could keep him from doing it.

One weekend I bought a beautiful photo frame decorated with faux jewels in my favorite colors: blue, teal, and green. I showed it to Bashir and told him how much I loved it. I couldn't wait to find the perfect picture to go in it. On Monday morning, I left the frame on my dresser before I went to work, and when I came home that evening, I discovered he had given it to one of his daughters as a gift.

When I asked him why he did that, he responded, "You want me to tell her to give it back?"

Another time, while working in the front yard, I told him how much I loved the tea olive shrub on our property. It was about five and a half feet tall and perfectly symmetrical, with glossy leaves and deliciously fragrant white flowers. It perfumed the entire front yard, and the aroma wafted into the garage. The next day, while I was at work, my husband hacked away at one side of the shrub.

When I came home, I immediately saw what he had done — the once symmetrical shrub looked like a half-moon — and asked him why. He said he felt it would "eventually" get too close to the house.

I tried to be a good Muslim wife. I wore a hijab and learned salat, the ritual Muslim prayer. I studied Arabic and went to the masjid, or mosque. I changed so much I no longer recognized myself.

One day when my husband was leading me in salat, I became distracted. I wanted to pray for guidance. I needed help dealing with the things that were bothering me. Bashir insisted that I focus on saying certain Arabic phrases in a specific way. My feet and toes had to point in a particular way; I had to keep my hands in a certain position. All of the attention to outward detail made me feel like I was performing an empty ritual. It wasn't an authentic prayer from my heart. Afterward, I asked Bashir if he really believed God would not hear my prayer if I held my hands and feet in the wrong position. Yes, he said, you must use the correct posture for your prayers to be answered.

His concept of God seemed small to me. Any God I worshipped would have to be bigger than that.

After that, I lost interest in praying, further straining our marriage. He would often talk — beaming with pride — about how he prayed. My approach to prayer didn't count.

You cannot talk to God if you do not call him Allah, Bashir insisted.

I thought it was odd that praying five times a day to Allah didn't make Bashir a better husband.

Neither Bashir's God nor my mother's God appealed to me. I thought serving God should make people more loving. I also thought it should empower people to grow, to become better. But their God was small, punitive, judgmental, and controlling — deities just like them.

As a child, I grappled with feelings of abandonment. My mother shunned me because I didn't embrace her religion. Why would she withhold her love because I didn't share her feelings or faith? The same truth applied to my marriage. I wanted my husband to love *me*, not the person he thought I should be.

It took me less than a year to realize I was stuck in a loop. But I waited nine years to file for divorce. During that time, my weight ballooned from 130 pounds to 218. My hair fell out. I was nearly bald at the crown. The skin on my face, shoulders, and back broke out horribly.

A naturopath ran tests on my organs. Biologically, my body functioned like an eighty-year-old woman, he said. I was in my early forties.

When I was younger, I liked to dress well. And, as I mentioned before, one inmate said to me at Dwight Correctional Center, "Every day, you dress like you're expecting a visit." Near the end of my marriage, I could barely recognize myself. I had become a sloppy-looking woman wearing a tent. My stress level was off the scale, and I felt like I was looking at death at an early age, but I still struggled to save my marriage. Divorce felt like failure. Of course, my tolerance for unhappiness was sky-high; it was all I had ever known.

In the end, it was too much. Bashir was unwell, too. Tending to his medical problems became a full-time job. He would have a seizure in the middle of the night, then come out of it not knowing his name or where he was. He would spend three or four days in the hospital after each seizure, and I was his only caretaker.

On top of that, the doctors discovered that Bashir had hepatitis B and C, probably from IV drug use during his younger days in Harlem. After fourteen years in prison, I did not want to be a full-time caregiver for a man who mistreated me and made excuses for his disrespectful daughters. I longed for a social life that wasn't limited to his interests, relatives, age group, and religion.

I wanted out.

ANSWERED PRAYER

Bashir and I had no real relationship. We were merely two people who shared space. We argued constantly. No matter what I said, he disagreed.

"Would it *hurt* you to agree with me some time?!" I screamed one evening. I stood at the kitchen sink, fixing my dinner plate. I often cooked dinner at five thirty in the morning, before I left for work. That way, my retired husband could eat early, as he preferred, and I ate alone when I got home twelve hours later. "Would it *cost* you something?"

Bashir feigned confusion.

"Why do you act like I'm the enemy?" I asked. "You argue with me about everything, but you don't do that with other people!"

Often, I heard my husband laughing and talking on the phone. He sounded like the nicest, happiest man in the world. "That's right, brother!" he would say. Or, "You got it, sister!" Then he would hang up the phone, walk out of the bedroom, and argue with me.

"You let people talk to you about me. You take their side and defend them against me!" I said. "I'm the one who takes care of you! Why do you act like I'm the enemy?"

One morning I shut off the alarm clock and trudged to the bathroom. I felt like an abandoned building. I slept sporadically. Grapefruit-sized tumors in my womb pressed on my bladder; I woke up and peed every hour or so.

I washed and combed my thinning hair. Early in my marriage, I wore a head wrap to cover my head because my husband was a Muslim and an imam. I wanted to respect his religion. Now I wore a wrap to cover my stress-induced baldness.

I shuffled to the kitchen. Bashir sat at the kitchen table in the breakfast nook, reading *The Atlanta Journal-Constitution*. He looked up and said, "*As-salaam alaikum*," Arabic for "Peace be unto you." Since I didn't speak Arabic and we didn't live peacefully, I ignored him.

I made coffee. I loved the aroma of fresh coffee, and the ritual always soothed me. But a nauseating stench rose from the sink. I kept a clean house. Why did the sink smell like something had crawled in it and died?

"What is that smell?" I asked.

Bashir said, "Yeah, I smell it, too." Big help.

I needed to dress for work, but the smell drove me crazy. I opened the cabinet under the sink and started unscrewing the pipes. My husband continued to read the paper. He did, however, tell me to shut the water off first. Once I separated the fittings, I placed a bucket beneath the main pipe. A misshapen, stinky mush spilled out — years of food caught in the lines. I cleared out the pipes, took them into the second bathroom, washed them out in the bathtub, and put everything back while my husband sat and watched.

I wrapped my hair, put on a long-sleeved blouse, and slid on an ankle-length green skirt with an elastic waistband that I wore at least twice a week. It was the most comfortable thing I had to accommodate my growing uterus and constantly expanding body. I walked past my husband, went into the garage, and started up the silver Honda Accord. I entered rush-hour traffic, drove for forty-five minutes, exited I-285, turned right, and pulled into the parking lot of the law firm where I worked. I was ten minutes late.

I sat at the front desk and looked at my calendar: September 24, 2009.

I called my husband. "Today is our ninth wedding anniversary."

"It is?"

"Yeah."

"We should celebrate this weekend."

"Okay, we'll see."

I hoped perhaps to see a "Happy Anniversary" card on the kitchen counter that evening. Nothing. I asked my husband whether he'd gotten me anything. "Nothing yet," he said. I asked him what he wanted to do on the weekend. He said, "I don't know." I went to bed.

On Saturday, I asked what we were going to do to celebrate our anniversary. "I'm not really into celebrating things," he said. I told him that our anniversary was important to me. After nine years together, I felt we should go somewhere. He ignored me.

The following week, I begged my husband to at least buy me a card. I needed him to acknowledge our years of marriage. The more I insisted, the more he resisted.

The following weekend, his daughter called to remind him that his eight-year-old grandson was having a birthday. "I'll stop by with a gift," he told her. "I want him to know it's from Pa-Pa." He hung up the phone, drove to Walmart, bought a gift, and drove an hour to his daughter's house.

He could have bought a card for me while he was in Walmart. He didn't. When he arrived home from his daughter's, he walked to the bedroom, stood in the doorway, and asked, "Did anybody call me?" Sprawled across the bed and staring at the ceiling fan, I ignored him. "Huh? Did anybody call me?" he persisted. "You hear me talking to you? Did anybody call me?" I continued to stare at the ceiling. He walked away, and I began to pray. "God, please help me get to a normal life. Please, God, help me get to a normal life. Please." I had been praying all my life, first to my mother's God, then to Bashir's God. But the plea for a normal life was the sincerest prayer I had ever uttered.

An hour or so later, I got up and walked into the living room. My husband sat on the sofa. He ate a piece of bean pie while watching a cable news program. I stood in front of the television, determined to be seen. He just chuckled and looked at me. I told him that I felt I should move in with one of my aunts for a while. He looked surprised but said, "Okay." He didn't ask me why. So, I proceeded to tell him.

I told him that he hurt me when he refused to celebrate our anniversary. I told him that people celebrate what they value, and if he had no interest in celebrating nine years of marriage, he didn't value our relationship. I told him that I resented the fact that he went out of his way to celebrate his grandson's birthday with a card and a gift but refused to do anything for me. "You value the members of your family more than me," I said.

He balled up his fists and threatened to punch me in the face. He had a habit of threatening me when he felt challenged, though he had never hit me. I wasn't going to wait for the first time. I called the police. I stood on the driveway to speak with arriving officers. I told them my husband was acting erratically. They told me to stay outside. They talked to Bashir inside the house, then came back out and spoke to me.

He could be developing behavioral difficulties due to his age, they said. They recommended that he see a doctor and filled out a report.

Bashir called a daughter and told her what had happened. She said he could stay at her house. He beamed like a happy child and told me, "I'm going to stay with my daughters! They want me to stay with them!" I had never seen him so excited. He packed a small bag and left. All of his daughters arrived in one car. "Bye!" he said, like a kid going to a sleepover. I suggested that his daughters take Bashir to a doctor. His oldest daughter, who was driving, nodded her head and said, "Yes, ma'am." I went inside and had the most restful night I'd had in months.

At work the next day, I checked my online bank balance and discovered that Bashir had raided our joint checking account. I called him and asked why he had taken out all of the money.

Instead of taking him to the doctor, his daughters had taken him to the bank. He said we would talk about it when I got home. We didn't. Once I got home, I discovered he had retrieved his medications and some clothes. He didn't leave a note, but it turned out he had gone to stay with one of his daughters, her husband, and their children.

I knew that this was the answer to my prayer. It was my opportunity to start a normal life.

After three days, I called him and asked if he was going to get the rest of his clothes. He said he didn't have anywhere to put them. I moved his things out of the master bedroom. I felt like I had been in a stale, shuttered room, and someone had just cracked a window.

We had no choice but to share our one car. I drove it to work during the week, and Bashir kept it on the weekends. If I needed to shop, I had to borrow it. On Sunday evenings, Bashir would drive to our house. I would then take him back to his daughter's house and keep the car for the workweek. It was a pain, but I needed a car because the public transportation system in Atlanta was terrible. In fact, it didn't exist in suburban Loganville.

Two months after Bashir moved out, I showed up ten minutes late for work. I sat at the reception desk, booted up the computer, and looked through work emails. The phone didn't ring much. Most clients knew the attorneys' direct numbers, so they didn't go through the receptionist. If a new client called, I put on my cheeriest voice and said, "Good afternoon, Wagner, Johnston, and Rosenthal!"

But there was something off this day. An hour after lunch, I got an email. David Johnston wanted me to come to his office. Pamela Jones, the legal secretary who was also the office manager, covered the front desk for me while I sat in David's office. Two of the firm's partners joined us.

"Lisa, come in and sit down," Johnston said.

I didn't know it that day in 2008, but the real estate market had crashed. The firm specialized in commercial real estate, and many of their clients had either gone bankrupt or were treading water.

"We've decided to lay you off," Johnston said.

He didn't say why, and I didn't ask. I sat there like an idiot. As part of my severance package, I stayed on the payroll and kept my health insurance for ninety days. When I went back to the front desk. Pam said, "Lisa, I'm so sorry this happened to you." I thanked her and went to the bathroom. By the time I came out, everyone had disappeared. There was no one to say good-bye to.

I called Bashir and told him what happened.

"Oh, well, you don't need the car anymore," he said. "I can use it."

As it turned out, my layoff was a gift. I qualified for unemployment benefits, and I didn't hesitate to draw them. Freed from work and a long commute, I focused on fixing my broken life.

REALLY OLD HURTS

At the end of my marriage, with the house to myself and no job, I found a way to deal with my pain. On the internet, I looked for stories and studies that would explain my situation. I found information on "life patterns," which led me to "patterns from childhood," which led me to "trauma."

Then I found the Emotional Freedom Technique, or EFT, an alternative treatment for physical pain and emotional distress. The treatment was also called tapping or psychological acupressure. Based on ancient Chinese medicine, EFT was not unlike the practice of acupuncture. Practitioners of both treatments believed that energy runs through the body along specific paths. A disruption in that energy was the cause of negative emotions and pain. Acupuncture relied on needles to address the breaks; EFT practitioners applied pressure to so-called hot spots or meridians with their fingertips.

I was intrigued. If blood runs through the body through veins and arteries, why not energy? When we experience pain or trauma the body remembers in the form of negative energy, EFT experts say. The negative energy produces physical, mental, and spiritual imbalances in our system, setting the stage for a wide variety of physical and emotional disorders. Tapping on these spots could release the negative energy stored in the body, creating emotional and physical healing.

Some studies showed that the practice could relieve post-traumatic stress disorder, anxiety, insomnia, headaches, depression, chronic pain, eating disorders, and phobias — all things I had suffered from at some point in my life. Research also showed that

EFT could improve brain function, change brain structure, and lay the foundation for achieving goals that had once seemed unachievable.

I was ready to try anything. I turned the room over the garage into my treatment center. The former home office had a hutch with a computer, a printer, supplies, a comfortable chair, and a writing desk. From a window, I could see anyone who approached the house. I turned on the house alarm system. If someone opened a door or a window downstairs, I would know it.

For the first few months after my husband left, I lived in that room. Each day I would make a meal — usually comfort food, like a big bowl of mac and cheese, or a grilled cheese sandwich and a cup of hot cocoa — and take my plate upstairs to the bonus room. I even slept on the carpeted floor. I wasn't used to having my own space, and I was quite comfortable living in just one room. I sat in front of the computer, got on the internet, and, for the first time, I did more than read about tapping: I started to tap.

I touched my face, arms, hands, and legs. I found a list of the basic parts of the body, identified via shorthand:

SH = Side of the Hand
EB = Eyebrow
SE = Side of the Eye
UE = Under the Eye
UN = Under the Nose
Ch = Chin
CB = Collarbone
UA = Under the Arm
WR = Wrists
TH = Top of the Head

Touching your body was only half the treatment. You had to state a specific problem or feeling associated with each body part.

The right statement was crucial. It helped you understand the issue. It produced clarity. It also helped soften the mind's resistance to change.

You had to love and accept yourself despite your issues. To begin, you said something like, "Even though I have this anger about something that happened, I completely love and accept myself anyway." You had to repeat your desire to heal three times while tapping the side of your hand. Next, you focused on a feeling, tied it to a part of your body, and rated the intensity of the feeling on a scale of one to ten. Using two to five fingers, you tapped firmly on parts of your body, repeating the exercise until the intensity level dropped to zero. Once the intensity was gone or greatly reduced, you could address other fears or emotions. You could peel them off in various layers, like an onion.

I found a website where a man named Brad Yates invited people to tap along with him, and I did. He offered a free download of his book, *The EFT Wizard's Big Book of Tapping Scripts: 101 Life-Enhancing, Fear-Smashing, Mind/Body-Healing, Abundance-Attracting, and Joy-Inspiring Rounds of EFT*. It was more than three hundred pages — and it promised a lot.

I downloaded the book, bought some paper, and printed it out. The scripts helped me find the right words while I tapped. At first, I was so emotionally blocked, I didn't know how to describe what I was feeling. Usually, whenever anyone asked how I was feeling, I just said, "Fine." I taped the scripts from Yates's book to the wall, along with a list of the body parts I needed to tap. The scripts had titles like "I'm Not Allowing Myself Good Feelings," "I Am Angry at Myself," and "I Have This Sadness About Not Being Good Enough."

I didn't revisit old hurts in chronological order. Instead, I leafed through the book and selected scripts at random, depending on how I was feeling. I had so little insight into what I needed that I embraced every script — all 101 of them, whether I thought it applied to me ("I've Got This Pain in My Knee") or not. I changed the words to make them fit my situation. I always had a pain somewhere.

The first script I used was called "I Have This Really Old Hurt." I tapped the side of my left hand with four fingers and said:

> *Even though I have this really old hurt,*
> *I choose to love and accept myself.*
> *Even though I have this really old hurt,*
> *I choose to love and forgive myself.*
> *Even though I have this really old hurt . . .*
> *Something happened a long time ago.*
> *I can't consciously remember it,*
> *but there's sadness.*
> *There's pain.*
> *There's anger,*
> *and it got stuck in me.*
> *And I choose to release it now.*
> *And even though I have this old hurt around my eyes,*
> *I choose to deeply and completely*
> *love and forgive and accept myself*
> *and anyone else who might have been involved in this*
> *because I choose to be free now.*

I tapped daily. Eventually, more personal things — things not in the book — came through. Suddenly the generic line about old hurt no longer felt right. After all, I had vivid, conscious memories from childhood, and I wanted to tap about them.

I called out specific hurts. "Even though my brother sexually molested me," I would say, or "Even though my mother treated me like crap."

Everything bubbled up.

Many of the scripts revolved around self-anger. None of them addressed being angry at someone else. After a few months, I began to talk about why I was angry. I tapped on my body and said I was angry about being molested by my brother for years. I was angry because my parents didn't keep me safe. I was angry because nobody was on my side. I was angry because my sisters and brothers were never wrong, and I was never right. I was angry because my siblings waited for me to do something wrong — anything, no matter how trivial — so they could tell our mother. I was angry because my family bullied me, and nobody helped me. I was angry because when I yelled "Stop!" as my brother groped, rubbed, and squeezed me, my parents looked at me with annoyance. I was angry because my mother, who was always quick to catch me in some alleged wrongdoing, never once asked my brother, *Whatchu doing?*

I tapped until I was physically and emotionally exhausted. I should have been gentler with myself, but I knew that my time alone was limited. I was drawing unemployment and had no money for a mortgage. To get a fresh start, I would have to move in with my parents in Chicago — but not yet.

In the beginning, I could barely get through the healing. I cried. I gagged. I coughed uncontrollably. I felt nauseous. My head ached; my vision blurred. Sometimes I could barely speak the words in the scripts. I pushed through and whispered them. Once I got the words out, I screamed. Memories flooded over me. I shouted at siblings who weren't there.

"Leave me alone!"

"Stop picking on me!"

I took two or three breaks, taking an hour to get through a ten-minute script. I would get to the end of a text and collapse on the floor, exhausted, only to wake up and realize that I had been asleep for hours. After some scripts, I would immediately run to the toilet. I drank a lot of water.

Eventually, I moved out of the bonus room. I slept on the sofa in the living room. I spread my scripts on the dining room table and taped others on the dining room wall. In prison, I could never tape anything on the wall, and when my husband lived in the house, he controlled the décor — and everything else. Being able to paper the wall and say my scripts out loud set me free. For the first time in my life, I felt I could do something I wanted to do. I was forty-three years old.

SURGERY

My body, meanwhile, was a mess. My uterus was so full of fibroids that I looked pregnant. When Wagner, Johnston & Rosenthal laid me off, they gave me a severance package that included health care and a salary for three months. I used the package to go under the knife in early 2010.

My surgery did not go as planned.

Bashir, still living with one of his daughters, was supposed to drive me to the hospital. That morning he showed up claiming not to feel well, so I drove to the hospital through the rush-hour traffic. Bashir sat in front and played backseat driver.

I focused on the operation ahead. My doctor, Thomas L. Lyons, who specialized in surgeries that left minimal scars, had received numerous awards for his breakthroughs in gynecologic surgery. He recognized that, just like the illnesses he treated, scars left by surgery could be debilitating. Since I often developed keloids after even the most minor injury, I felt that I was in good hands.

A second surgeon, a woman, joined Dr. Lyons in the operating room. She held my hand as the anesthesiologist put me to sleep. This time I just drifted off — there was no out-of-body experience. I looked at the surgeon and told her that she was very comforting. "That's why she's here!" Dr. Lyons said. She smiled, and I heard other people chuckling.

When I came to, I learned he had performed a hysterectomy and had also removed my left ovary. When the doctor finally came into my room he explained to me that he had no choice.

Once the camera was inside me, he said he could see that a polyp had been hiding beneath the large fibroids. There was also a fibroid hanging from my left ovary. A blood vessel as thick as his index finger fed it. Up until that time, he said, I had lost very little blood during the surgery — an important factor since the operation had been postponed twice while the doctors tried to get my blood iron count up. In the end, he said, it was safer for him to remove the ovary than try to remove the fibroid and risk nicking the blood vessel, which would trigger a massive blood loss.

He said he remembered my fear of being left with a giant keloid, and he considered that during the surgery. So instead of removing my uterus through one large incision, he removed my uterus, my left ovary, all the fibroids, and the polyp by cutting them into tiny pieces and pulling them out through a small incision underneath my navel.

The surgery took five hours.

Later that evening, the female surgeon came to see me. She told me that she had watched Dr. Lyons every step of the way and that she was pleased with the outcome.

"I have no reason to say this unless it was true," she said. "Dr. Lyons was on top of his game with you."

After seeing my uterus, she and Dr. Lyons had had a long discussion about whether to perform a hysterectomy. Since I had indicated that my family was complete, they felt a hysterectomy was in my best interest. They could have removed the fibroids and left my uterus. But my uterus was mostly all fibroids. The little muscle tissue that would have been left would have been very weak, and my uterus could easily burst later, she said.

"We don't want to see you back here in a year having an emergency surgery to remove a ruptured uterus, when we could remove it safely now," she told me.

I was sad, but I believed her. Mostly I was glad that they did everything through a very tiny incision, rather than open me up to save time.

The doctor hugged me and said she would come back and see me the next day.

A nurse came in and asked how I felt. I told her that I had a headache and asked for a cup of coffee with cream and sugar. She stared at me. It was the first time anyone had asked for a cup of coffee after waking up from surgery, she said.

"I have to write this down," she said.

I stayed in the hospital for two nights. On the morning of my release, I called Bashir, who had promised to drive me home.

"Where are you?" I asked.

"Asleep," he said.

"Bashir, they're ready to release me. I need you to get me."

"Look, don't rush me," he said. "I've had a terrible couple of days."

"You've had a terrible couple of days?"

"Yes."

"Bashir, I'm the one who had surgery!"

He arrived hours later and drove me to my aunt Amie's home in Marietta, where I spent two nights recuperating. After that, I was ready to sleep in my own bed. Bashir picked me up and drove me home.

Although I believed the hysterectomy was necessary, I still struggled to accept the surgery's outcome. Dr. Lyons had removed parts of my body without my explicit consent. Even though I kept arriving at the conclusion that I agreed with his decision, my emotions were in turmoil. I could not shake the feeling that something bad had happened to me, although I couldn't put my finger on why I felt that way. I was undoubtedly healthier without my uterus. The fact I couldn't get pregnant again didn't bother me, and I didn't feel like I had lost my identity as a woman. Instead, the nagging feeling was one of being violated, again. The surgery's outcome reminded me of my mother, who threw away my things when I was gone.

"It's done now," she would say.

I kept tapping.

DIVORCE

After the surgery, I ordered *Nolo's Essential Guide to Divorce* from Amazon.com. When it came in the mail, I threw it on the bed and cried. Even after all the misery I had endured, the thought of divorce broke my heart. The book said I would feel sad, confused, and conflicted. It also said getting a divorce is a fairly straightforward process.

After a few days, I typed up the forms and mailed them to the Walton County Courthouse in Monroe, Georgia. When Bashir came over a few days later, I handed him a copy of the papers. His face briefly registered surprise, but then he recovered and said nothing. Neither of us hired a lawyer. We appeared in court once. I arrived alone; Bashir came with all of his daughters.

I didn't want to stay in Georgia. I wanted to sell the house. But Bashir convinced me that it made sense for us to keep the house since he planned to stay, and said he'd pay the mortgage.

I called the mortgage company to see if Bashir could refinance the loan in his name. It wasn't the best time to negotiate. The real estate market had collapsed. Still, mortgage companies like CitiMortgage had developed programs to help people avoid foreclosure. I had just been laid off, so I used that as an argument for getting into one of those programs. However, every time I called CitiMortgage, they acted like they had never heard of me. I stayed on the phone for forty-five minutes answering questions posed by a company representative. After hearing nothing for weeks, I followed up — only to be told the company had no record of my earlier call. After weeks of getting the runaround, I told Bashir, "If you want to keep the house, *you* need to talk to these people."

I loaded a rented van with everything I had paid for: a dinette set, the living room sectional, pictures on the wall, a beautiful mirror above the fireplace, a bench and table in the foyer. I tossed in my mixer, bread maker, and other kitchen appliances and drove everything to a consignment shop in Marietta. I stored a few things in an aunt's basement, mostly books, but also a landscape painting I liked. Back at home, I tossed a mattress on the living room floor in front of the television. That's where I ate and slept.

I threw everything else away, including mismatched plates and bowls and my bathroom decorations.

I threw away one last thing: my wedding dress, which I had kept in a plastic sleeve in the back of the closet.

In March 2010, two months after my hysterectomy, I bought a one-way plane ticket to Chicago. I removed the tapping scripts on the walls in the house and packed all of my belongings that I had left into a single piece of carry-on luggage.

Bashir came to the house that morning, drove me to the Hartsfield-Jackson airport, and then moved back into our house.

A few hours later, I landed at Midway airport in Chicago. Once a proud homeowner, I now slept on a lumpy futon in the living room of my parents' apartment. I was home — again. One morning I sat on the futon and cried. I had worked so hard to rebuild my life. After ten years, I had nothing to show for it.

book three

Colorado

DENVER

After a few months of living with my parents, I was ready to be on my own again. Over the past ten years I had changed a lot, and it was awfully hard to live with people who had changed very little.

I still had a lot of unresolved issues, but the work I had done in Georgia began to pay off. I was calmer and more controlled. I was ready to leave Chicago and my past.

I moved to Colorado, where Gary Cox, whom I'd met through the IWW while I was in Dwight Correctional Center, lived with his wife, Carol.

I stayed in their condo, sleeping on an air mattress on the floor of their open loft. They made sure I had a little fun — something I hadn't had in years. We went to Red Rocks Park and Amphitheatre, an open-air historic concert venue built into a rock structure in Morrison, Colorado, about ten miles west of Denver. They introduced me to Good Times Burgers & Frozen Custard. Since the restaurant only operates in Colorado and Wyoming, I had never heard of it. I thought their food was delicious. Plus, I was hungry not only for burgers but also for any new experience, no matter how small. Gary and Carol also took me to the Denver Museum of Nature & Science and to family dinners with their adult children and grandchildren.

Living with them gave me a comfortable space to lay my head, get my bearings, and look for a job. I was grateful.

I stayed with them for six weeks. Admittedly, that was a long time. Too long. So long, in fact, that people were starting to talk.

One day one of their adult sons came to visit. I said hello from upstairs in the loft where I slept, and then stayed upstairs, not wanting to intrude upon the son's time with his parents. At one point, I heard the son ask if I was just going to stay there and live off them. Gary said, "Oh no, she wants to be independent!"

I sat in the loft above them, listening, and asking myself, *Are they talking about me?* I was confused. I had money. I was still getting unemployment benefits via direct deposit to my checking account. I bought food and soap and other items for my friend's condo, and I had all of my own personal supplies. Whenever I would try to pay for meals or the like, Carol would say, "Keep your money, you're going to be needing it." I didn't feel like I was there because I wasn't independent. I was offended that my friend was allowing his adult children to think that I was there living off their parents. I didn't feel like I was doing that. I thought I was there as a visitor, at their invitation. And I spent the better part of every day outside of their home, signing up with employment agencies and actively looking for work. I tried to give them their personal space.

That was the beginning of a change in my relationship with them.

About a week later, while Carol was at the grocery store, Gary suggested we have sex. I refused, and he exploded, yelling and cursing and accusing me of just being there to use him. Thanks to my tapping, I didn't respond with a sense of imminent doom or danger. I didn't overreact or irrationally seek to defend myself. Instead, I left his house and called his wife. I told her what had happened.

Carol was mortified, but she thought it would probably be best if I could find my own place soon.

A TEMPORARY LIFE

Two days later, Gary and Carol drove me to a Motel 6 north of Denver. I was still getting a weekly unemployment check, and I had managed to save a few hundred dollars. Gary and Carol drove into the parking lot, and I saw my new home: a motel next to I-25, a major highway that joined Santa Fe, Denver, and Cheyenne. Gary sat in their car behind the wheel and waited while Carol and I went into the front office. I had reserved a room online, so the check-in process was short. The clerk made a copy of my Georgia driver's license and handed me a plastic key card. She whispered my room number to me so that no one else in line would know it. Then Carol and I got back in the car. We drove around in circles looking for the room, only to discover that it was so close to the front office that it would have been easier to have walked to it. Finally, Gary pulled up the car right in front of my room and parked. I opened my door, grateful that the key card worked the first time, then carried my few belongings inside and placed them on the bed. Carol said, "oh, too bad there's no refrigerator. Maybe you can move to another room." I said, "no, it'll be fine." Gary and Carol looked in the bathroom and commented that at least everything was clean. After about ten minutes I hugged Carol, and then Gary, and told them I would let them know how I was doing. And then they left.

I felt nothing but relief. It was a budget motel room, but it was mine. I had my own space again, something I hadn't had since leaving Georgia, and desperately needed. Every time I lived with other people, even with my parents or my husband, I felt like I could not be myself. I felt like I was always being monitored and judged, whether anyone was actually doing it or not. I only felt free when I was alone. Living in a motel had its perks. A young Mexican woman cleaned my room every Tuesday afternoon, which made me feel taken care of, in a strange way. She didn't speak much English, but she was very friendly. And I liked seeing the same woman every week. I would always give her a two-dollar tip.

My room had a queen-size bed, a small sofa, and a little round table with a chair where I could sit and write — although I almost always sat on my bed, just like I had in prison. I could adjust the air-conditioning and the heat, and there was cable TV. One wall was orange, my favorite color. The curtains on the window were red, which was my second-favorite color. There was a small coin laundry near the office. There were three washing machines on the left, and three dryers on the right. It seemed like at least one washing machine and one dryer was always out of service. In between was a small wooden table where people folded their laundry. I kept a couple of rolls of quarters at all times and washed and dried my clothes just after sunrise, when the laundry room was empty. There were fax and photocopying services available at the front office, and they would hold my mail for me. Also, since I didn't own much except a few clothes — a few pairs of slacks, some blouses, a couple of casual suit jackets that I could mix and match with my slacks and wear to work, and a winter coat — the room was just the right size for me. My prized possession was my laptop. I used it to search for a job. I always put it under the mattress whenever I left the room. Fortunately, the motel had free Wi-Fi in all the rooms — and free coffee in the front office. The staffers in the front office were always courteous and willing to assist me, which made me feel accepted and respected in a way I hadn't felt in a long, long time — if ever. After a few days I realized that it actually would have been nicer to have had a refrigerator. I asked someone at the front desk if there was any way that I could get a room with a fridge, but the only ones available were on the second floor, and farther from the front office. I didn't want to move. Living alone, I did prefer to live on higher floors, where there was less chance of someone climbing through the window, but in this case, it was more important to live close to the front office — just in case anything happened. I was always thinking about needing to feel safe. It had nothing to do with my physical location. Since childhood I had always had a constant, general feeling that I was never safe, that at any minute something bad might happen. It was less than a two-minute walk from my room to the check-in desk, which was open twenty-four hours a day. That for me outweighed any safety I might have felt living on a higher floor. I bought a small foam cooler and filled it with ice from the machine in the front office. My room faced the parking lot. If I opened my window, I could hear children laughing and playing in the outdoor pool (which didn't bother me), but I couldn't see the pool from my window, and I never wanted to get in it.

Other than that, the motel was surprisingly quiet. I had no trouble sleeping at night. There were the occasional sounds of people getting in and out of their cars in the parking lot. And every once in a while, I could hear the noises of couples who had clearly rented the room next door just for a couple of hours. But none of that bothered me, either. I was focused on my own life.

I continued to tap. I no longer needed a script, but the work got harder. Each session ended with a feeling of relief — and the realization that I needed to go deeper. The improvement was real, but it was gradual.

My body responded. My jaws unclenched. It took longer, though, for my fists to do the same. One day, while standing at the mirror getting dressed for work, I noticed that, while I didn't feel angry, I looked angry. My body was communicating something that my mind wasn't ready to hear.

I made a conscious decision to focus on anger, even though part of me denied I felt that way. Later, I discovered that chronic anger often masks a deep well of sadness. But I wasn't ready to go there yet. I had to heal. And I had to focus on surviving in Colorado, where I was alone and living just above broke. I couldn't afford to be sad. And somehow, feeling angry felt more powerful than feeling sad.

I was getting jobs through temp agencies and commuting for hours, so I could only tap in the evenings and on weekends. Often, I was too tired to tap at night. But I made time to tap on Saturdays and Sundays. I was better in a lot of ways, but I still suffered. I knew my journey into wholeness was not yet complete.

I knew that it would be a long time before I got back to Chicago. I called my parents and gave them the address of the motel. I didn't tell them why I had really left Gary and Carol's house. I said that I wanted to have some space of my own. "I can understand that," my mother said. Then I called my daughter, who was also still in Chicago with her new husband. Bashir and I had driven more than eleven hours from our home in Loganville to Chicago, and we had been part of the wedding ceremony. I updated my daughter on my move. I told everybody that I was "fine." I was divorced and living in a motel room, alone and far from home, but I didn't want anybody feeling sorry for me.

I had no car. I walked everywhere: to the Village Inn restaurant (which was on the Motel 6 property), Santiago's (for the chicken fajitas), Burger King, Popeye's, and the Save-A-Lot grocery store. In the morning, I walked to the bus stop, a half-hour hike, to get to work. I spent another twenty minutes on a bus heading downtown for an assignment.

When I applied for a temporary or permanent job, I assumed the employment agencies and employers would run a background check on me. I never told them I was a felon, or that I had spent years in prison. I never got turned down by an employment agency, and I never had a problem with the background check. I always signed up with the agencies online, and I always checked "no" on the application where it asked if I had ever been convicted of a crime.

Why ruin my chances of getting a job? They would discover what they discovered, and I was never sure why I passed scrutiny. My primary goal was always to keep the roof over my head. Whenever I got an assignment, I would sit on my bed in my motel room, take out a piece of paper, and calculate how many days I would have to work to earn what I needed to pay for my room that week. The rent at Motel 6 was cheaper if I could pay for the week instead of by the day, so each week I was working just to pay the rent, first. With what money I had left, I could buy some bread, lunch meat, cheese, and chips and have a sandwich for lunch and dinner.

Most of the jobs I got were in law firms; I had signed up with agencies that specialized in that niche. I thought it was the best use of a paralegal certificate, and I really wanted to land a full-time job using it. The jobs were mostly for a couple of days — sometimes a week. Others were indefinite. Most days I had to be at work at 9:00 A.M., and so I usually left my room at about 7:15.

At the end of the day, I made the same trek in reverse, taking two buses to get from downtown Denver to the Thornton Park-n-Ride, and then walking twenty minutes from the Park-n-Ride to my room at Motel 6. I did this five days a week — rain, shine, sleet, or snow. I always left in plenty of time to make sure that I didn't miss the bus. And the bus was always crowded. By the time I boarded it was standing room only. I had a winter coat that I had brought with me from Chicago, but the weather was warm. What I really needed — and didn't have — was an ankle-length raincoat. It seemed like every day, just as I left work, a thundercloud would form directly over my head and drench me. I bought an umbrella, but with the wind blowing the rain sideways, it wasn't enough to keep my entire body dry. And every day that this happened, I'd arrive at my motel room soaked from just above my kneecaps down to my shoes. I struggled with the Colorado climate. I'd gotten used to Georgia's humidity. Despite the fact that July 2010 was a wet month for Denver, with an almost daily rain shower that started as soon as I left work, the air in Denver was extremely dry compared with Georgia. My lips cracked, my hair and nails broke off, and my skin felt like a potato chip.

Because I walked so much during the week, on my off days, I just wanted to rest. I'd go out only to get something to eat, and then I'd stretch out on my bed and watch TV. I never saw anybody at the motel that I wanted to date, although occasionally men attempted to flirt with me. I would see the same people paying their rent in the front office when I went to pay mine. I wasn't the only one living there long-term. In fact, a woman in the front office told me there was a man who had been there for two years. Sometimes men would strike up a conversation with me, either in the laundry room or as I walked to and from my room. They would usually start with "Are you living here by yourself?" and end with "Can I get your phone number? Maybe we can go out sometime." I never gave anybody my phone number. Once the phone in my room rang in the middle of the night. I answered it and a man's voice asked me if I wanted to date. I hung up the phone without answering him, and he (whoever he was) didn't call back. I didn't have the energy to even think about a relationship. I certainly wasn't interested in any one-night stands with strangers. And, right or wrong, I presumed that nobody I met at a Motel 6 was likely to be a good candidate for a long-term relationship. Looking back, I suppose there could have been single men there who were doing just what I was doing — starting over. But at the time, I saw a relationship as a distraction from what I needed to concentrate on: myself.

I worked temporary jobs for about six months and seldom saw another Black person at work. One of my long-term assignments (a few months) was at a law firm called Snell & Wilmer located in the Tabor Center in downtown Denver. I worked in the records office as a records management assistant. The firm had recently implemented a new database. My official duties were described as being responsible for records classification, indexing, retention, and hold management using Accutrac Records Management Software. My reality was a large conference room almost completely filled with file boxes that I was to carry, either by hand or stacked on a dolly, to the closet-sized space they had set up as my workstation. There I would take each individual file out of a box, enter the information on the paper files into the electronic file system, save the electronic file, and put the paper file back into the box. Then I would move to the next file in the box, until I had completed the box — which usually contained about fifty files. After I had finished one box, I set it aside and repeated the process with another box. After I had processed two or three boxes, I would either load them back onto the dolly or carry them individually, by hand, to a large file room located down the hall and make sure that the boxes were arranged alphabetically.

Since they weren't alphabetical when I got them, putting them in their final home in alphabetical order required constant jostling of the boxes that were already there. It was entry-level, largely manual work, and I did it alone. I seldom saw another person, except when the records office manager popped in to see how things were going. "Everything okay?" she'd ask every day. "Oh yes, everything is fine," I would answer. "Good, good," she would say. "Let me know if you need anything." And that was pretty much it.

The only thing I liked about that job was that having learned a records management system would look good on my résumé. Other than that, Snell & Wilmer was spread out over three floors in the building, and I was essentially relegated to its basement.

I wasn't making much money, even though I had a paralegal certificate and a bachelor's degree. After the agencies took their cut, I earned between $10 and $12 an hour. But some of the jobs promised full-time work, and I knew that if I could get my foot in the door and get hired somewhere, I could negotiate a better salary

for myself. Strange as it seems, it was a happy and exciting time. I
was on my own, with my future ahead of me.

When I had indexed and filed all the boxes in the records office
at Snell & Wilmer, the assignment was over, and I went on to the
next one. I had gotten another assignment, Special Counsel at
Winzenburg, Leff, Purvis & Payne, through a different employment agency. They needed someone for a few weeks to cover for a
woman who was getting married and going on a honeymoon. The
firm represented homeowner associations — townhomes and
condominiums included — throughout the state of Colorado. My
co-workers were nice enough. But twice a day, once at 10:00 A.M.
and once at 2:00 P.M., mail was delivered to the front desk. I had to
stop what I was doing, grab a little buggy, pick up the mail at the
front desk, and sort it at my desk. Then I had to push this little
buggy around for thirty to forty-five minutes, delivering mail to
the offices of everyone in the firm. I felt humiliated. I almost never
felt like what I was doing was beneath me, but something about
pushing that little buggy around while knowing that I had a paralegal certificate and a bachelor's degree in business administration
just gnawed at me. I couldn't stand it. I couldn't wait to get out of
there. The attorneys and other staff in the office were friendly. In
the few weeks that I was there, I tried to be as pleasant as possible,
but I felt like I was doing work that one of their teenage children
could have done as a summer job.

One day I got a phone call from an agency called Rossi Staffing.
Connie Rossi called my Tracfone and said she had a temp-to-perm
position open that she thought I would be able to fill. If I could
have turned a cartwheel, I would have.

While I was still working at Winzenburg, Leff, Purvis & Payne,
Connie sent me on an interview at Temkin, Wielga & Hardt. I
went during my lunch break. The attorneys at Temkin, Wielga &
Hardt specialized in environmental and natural resources, litiga-
tion, intellectual property, and international law. I knew nothing

about their specialized field. For the past six months, I had been carrying boxes and pushing buggies. Patti Pringle, the office administrator, a six-foot-tall blonde who appeared to be in her mid- to late fifties, met me at the Common Grounds Coffeehouse, two blocks from the firm's offices. I was being interviewed for a position that was not exactly open. They were planning to fire the person who had the job but didn't want to fire her before they found her replacement. Patti bought both of us a cup of coffee, and we talked for about an hour about my skills and about what they were looking for. Connie had prepared me well for the interview. I made sure that I described what I brought to the table in a way that exactly matched what they needed. I think you will be a great assistant for Mark, Patti said. He's the one you will be working with every day. I'm going to see when he can meet with you.

Attorney Mark Wielga interviewed me a few days later. Mark was about five foot ten, with salt-and-pepper hair. He was dressed casually in slacks and a short-sleeved shirt. He had an easygoing manner about him, with an easy laugh and a warm demeanor. He also ran a nonprofit research organization called NomoGaia. It was an organization that helped governments and international institutions understand how their business practices affected their workers' human rights. I was impressed. I really wanted the job. This second interview went extremely well, but Mark said I had to have a third interview with Betsy Temkin, the firm's managing partner. Nobody got hired unless Betsy approved, but my interview with her felt more like a formality.

Shortly after my interviews, Temkin, Wielga & Hardt hired me in November 2010. I started on a sixty-day probationary period, during which I would still be working for Rossi Staffing. If things worked out, the law firm promised to hire me. Thirty days later, Mark said there was no reason to make me wait the full sixty days. The firm hired me as a full-time permanent employee with benefits. I was on cloud nine. I would finally be able to get an apartment.

Before I filled out the final employment paperwork, I went to the Social Security office in downtown Denver and changed my last name from my married name, Bashir, back to my maiden name, Forbes. The name Bashir belonged to a man from whom I was determined to make a clean break. And I wasn't a Muslim, so I didn't want to keep an Arabic name. I wanted to be free to say who I was. My name was Lisa Forbes.

PARLIAMENT

No longer living off a temporary job, I was ready to stop having a temporary home. I wanted a place to call my own. I wanted to be able to decorate and to cook. I called Housing Helpers and told them I needed a place that was near either a bus stop or a train station so I could get back and forth from downtown. I also wanted a place near a grocery store. And I wanted a place that was reasonably safe for a woman on her own. A woman at Housing Helpers recommended an apartment complex called Parliament Apartments.

I checked out their website. The complex, at 4363 South Quebec Street, stood near the intersection of I-25 and I-225, near Belleview Station, a light rail stop. "Denver's Downtown fun and the metro area are just minutes from our beautiful renovated one- and two-bedroom homes," the site said. "Each apartment features expansive living rooms, bedrooms with walk-in closets and attached baths, new kitchens with stainless appliances, granite countertops, and more. Our community offers a heated swimming pool and hot tub, a clubhouse, a 24-hour fitness center, Wi-Fi in common areas, controlled access, additional storage, garage parking, and more — all in a pet-friendly, conveniently located community! Enjoy the city's best shopping, dining, education, business, recreation, and entertainment just a short distance from your new home, too."

It sounded perfect. The next Saturday morning I got up early. While it was still dark outside, I went to the front desk at Motel 6 and got my usual two Styrofoam cups of coffee, stirred two packs of cream and two packs of sugar into each cup, and walked back to my room, being careful not to spill anything. The trick was opening the door while holding the coffee cups, because I never wanted to set my cups on the ground. I always managed to make it happen — a small success that I celebrated every morning. As soon as it was light outside, I walked twenty minutes to the first of three buses that I had to take to get from Motel 6 to Parliament Apartments. The third bus let me off a block from the apartment complex. By the time I got there, I was tired but excited. The people at the leasing office greeted me warmly and gave me a tour of the premises. I applied for a one-bedroom, one-bathroom apartment.

I had saved the $500 security deposit, and I just barely met the minimum credit score of 600. My name was still on the mortgage on the house in Georgia I had shared with my ex-husband; he was still living there and making monthly payments.

Still, I worried: Would I pass the background check? I had changed my name at the Social Security office, but I hadn't changed my ID. I filled out the application using my married name, and held my breath. They ran the background check on Lisa Bashir, and it came back clean. I exhaled. They told me that I could move in the next Saturday.

I filled out the rest of the paperwork and rode the three buses back to Motel 6. Having no one in Colorado to celebrate with, I called my parents in Chicago to tell them about it. I instantly knew my mother wasn't home when my father answered the phone.

"Hello?"

"Hi, Daddy! It's Lisa!"

"Hi, sugar plum! How's everything?"

Daddy always called us sugar plum, honey babe, or honey bunny — unless he was angry. Then he called us by our names. If he was upset with something that one of us did and he was talking to my mother about it, he would say to her, "Well, that's your child!" And he always called my mother honey — again, unless he was angry. Then he'd call her Mrs. Forbes.

Daddy knew that I'd been living at Motel 6 because I had given my parents my new address when I left Gary and Carol's house.

I told him that I had just gotten approved for an apartment, and that it was a very nice place. I would be moving on Saturday.

"Oh you got one!" he said. "I'm proud of you, honey babe! I'll be sure to tell Mama you called!"

"Okay, love you, Daddy!"

"Love you, too, honey bunny!"

Still smiling, I hung up the phone.

I didn't call home often. I mostly called when I had good news, or if something significant happened — like a change of address.

The call with my father was brief, but it was enough. I wanted him to be proud of me. And he was.

Later I called Gary and Carol and gave them an update on what was going on. They offered to help me move into my apartment, and I jumped at the opportunity to not have to drag everything I owned — not that it was much — onto three buses to move.

A week later, on October 16, 2010, I piled my few belongings into black garbage bags, put them into the trunk of Gary and Carol's car, and went to the check-in desk at Motel 6 — this time to check out for good. After months of motel living, I said good-bye to the familiar people behind the front desk and hello to a place of my own.

My second-floor apartment was 489 square feet. The living room window overlooked the parking lot. And while I had never seen her, I believed the woman who lived above me worked nights. Every night at 3:00 A.M. like clockwork, I was awakened by heels loudly clicking on the hardwood floors overhead. I asked the managers if they could ask her to remove her shoes when she came in at night. The clicking stopped. A new sound emerged. A dog or a cat seemed to be running back and forth from the living room window to the bedroom all night long. The sound of paws resounded across the hardwood floors, and I seldom got a full night's sleep unless I wore headphones.

The only bathroom was inside my bedroom. Guests sleeping in the living room would have had to enter my bedroom at night to use the bathroom. Fortunately (or sadly), I never had that problem. I liked the fact that the apartment was equipped with a stackable washer and dryer. I didn't like the fact that the washer and dryer were located inside my clothes closet, which was inside the bathroom, which was inside my bedroom. Worse, the washing machine leaked when I used it. Every time I walked into the closet, water squirted up from the floorboards. I complained constantly about the water, and the maintenance workers assured me they had fixed it. The problem never went away.

The garbage disposal didn't work, either. Every night I would thoroughly clean my kitchen sink. And every morning I would find garbage in the sink that clearly had backed up from what I assumed was the apartment above me. I didn't eat the kinds of food that appeared in my own sink. I was revolted, and though I complained multiple times to management and they kept promising to fix it, they never did.

I rode this merry-go-round for the two and a half years that I lived in that apartment. I should have made a scene, but I felt like I was lucky to have someplace to live.

Black spots appeared on the walls. I wiped them away with Lysol, but they would always come back. I didn't know what mold was. I didn't connect the spots to my irritated eyes and frequent headaches. I often had trouble breathing while at home, and I developed a chronic itchy skin rash. I attributed all of this to Colorado's dry air.

I focused on living a quiet life, working full-time, trying to stay under the radar, and decorating my apartment and making it feel like home. I bought a red Mr. Coffee coffeemaker to brighten up my kitchen. That small red countertop appliance created a feeling of "flow" in the apartment, because the living room — which was open to the kitchen — had a red accent wall. The rest of the walls were painted beige.

Dimitri Vanderbellen, who happened to be a Scientologist, gave me furniture for my new place. I met him in 2013, on the evening before Thanksgiving. He was in the leasing office when I stopped by after work with a maintenance request. He was offering free facials to show people the line of skin care products that he sold, but no one was taking him up on it. I suggested it was probably because people were traveling for Thanksgiving. He said he hadn't thought about that, and he offered to give me a free facial. I was just getting off work and was tired so I declined and asked for a rain check. He gave me several samples to take with me, which, surprisingly, cleared up my eczema. After that I began ordering skin care products from him.

One day, when he delivered my order to my door, I invited him in and he realized that I didn't have any furniture. He said he had a futon and a full-size bed frame and mattress in storage and that if I wanted them, I could have them for free. The only catch was that I would have to help him carry them up the stairs to my apartment. I considered that a bargain since I was tired of sleeping on a pallet on the floor. I mean, even in Motel 6 I had had a bed. We got the futon and the bed into my apartment, and Dimitri put everything together for me. I went out and bought some sheets and a had a great night's sleep on my new used bed.

A small island with space underneath for storing pots and pans separated the living room from the kitchen. Since I could eat at the island, I didn't have a table. I ordered two dark wooden breakfast barstools from Walmart.com. I seldom ate breakfast before I left for work. Usually all I had time for was a cup of coffee before I had to run for the bus. I always seemed to be running late. In the evenings, when I came home from work, I ate what most people would consider breakfast — scrambled eggs with toast and jelly, or a bowl of cereal. On the weekends I would cook chicken and some macaroni and cheese, or spaghetti. Although I liked to cook, after nearly ten years of marriage, I wasn't used to cooking for one. So, I ate a lot of pizza, which I would buy at the grocery store and bring home to bake in the oven.

I found two inexpensive pictures to hang on the accent wall above the futon — landscapes, with scenes of trees and water. The landscapes were soothing, but that wasn't the main reason I bought them. I bought them because I didn't like pictures or artwork with strangers' faces hanging on the walls. I had some pictures of family members, but they were in a photo album. And that's where I left them.

When I wasn't at work, I was mostly alone. I started to feel like I wanted to have some kind of a social life. I spent some time with Dimitri, but our relationship was platonic. Dimitri liked to take me to events at the Church of Scientology of Colorado, which happened to be located only four blocks from my job. I wanted to meet people, but I didn't want to be roped into another religion. I tried Meetup.com and joined every group I could find. My ex-husband had introduced me to old movies starring actors like Cary Grant, Ingrid Bergman, Orson Welles, Humphrey Bogart, and Katharine Hepburn, and Turner Classic Movies became one of my favorite cable TV channels. The scenes in old films were so elegant, and the actors were always well dressed, like I longed to be. I loved movies like *To Catch a Thief, Citizen Kane, Gaslight, Casablanca,* and *Arsenic and Old Lace* (which was funny). The old films could be romantic without having gratuitous or explicit sex scenes. Romance and elegance were what I wanted. When I saw that there were clubs for people who liked to watch old movies, I eagerly joined one, hoping to meet someone there to go out with — only to be embarrassed when I discovered that everyone came with a partner.

There were meetups for people who liked to travel. I dreamed of traveling, but I didn't have any money, so I stopped going. There were plenty of book clubs, too, but none of them were reading books that I wanted to read. In prison I had developed a love of

classical literature, and I wanted to read more of it. Most of the
book clubs seemed to be reading popular fiction, and it really
wasn't my style. I'd been forced to study the Jehovah's Witnesses'
magazines and books for years. I didn't want to read things that
didn't interest me just to be part of a group. There was even a
meetup for people who liked to play softball — I don't know what
I was thinking when I joined that one. Over time, I calmed down
and dropped every group but the chess club. I didn't know how to
play chess when I joined the club, but I didn't have to. They had
lessons for beginners. I loved the game for the same reason that I
loved math: It was logical and orderly, two things my mind craved.

I continued to struggle with issues tied to my past. At work Mark
Wielga's calm voice and steady personality soothed me, and I got
along with him in every way. But I felt irritated by other people
with authority over me — administrators, managing partners, and
senior attorneys — even when they were nice people. Any whiff of
control triggered feelings of intense resistance in me. I disliked
being dominated. If a supervisor didn't approach me in the right
way, I bristled and felt disrespected. I did top-notch work, but I
was defensive and often abrasive. On some level, I still only felt safe
when I kept people at a distance. I trusted no one.

I felt like my co-workers (stand-ins for my siblings) were talking
about me to the attorneys (stand-ins for my parents), competing
with me for no apparent reason, undermining me, deliberately
making it seem like something was wrong with me. I never felt
like I was accepted. There were three legal secretaries in the firm:
me; a white woman, Gina, about my age; and a Hispanic woman,
Andrea, in her late twenties or early thirties. But there wasn't
much camaraderie. People seemed competitive; they vied to be
the "favorite." One time Gina told Patti, the office administrator,
that I didn't work as hard as the other assistants. They each got
work from two attorneys, and I only supported Mark, who was
often out of the office. But that perspective didn't factor in that I

was doing things that they weren't doing. Even on this job, I *still* was the one who had to go downstairs and check the mail every day, sort it, and deliver it to each attorney's assistant. I was responsible for making coffee first thing in the morning and whenever the pot was empty, for ordering supplies for the break room and the copy room, for making sure the printers and copiers always had paper in them, and for making sure the kitchen was clean and the dishwasher was turned on at the end of the day. I also was responsible for keeping the library up to date. When new editions of law books arrived, it was my job to remove the old editions from the library and put the new editions on the shelf. And when there was any need for a maintenance call (for instance, if the attorneys thought heating or cooling systems weren't working properly), I had to make sure that the problem got solved. And I also picked up any overflow work if the other assistants were super busy. So even though Mark traveled a lot, it wasn't as if I had nothing to do when he was gone. I still worked hard and made my contribution to the office.

I had thought my full range of responsibilities was obvious to others. Now, with Gina's comment to Patti, I felt like I had to prove and defend myself.

A couple of years after I was hired, Andrea resigned, and the firm hired a Black woman to replace her. I thought that would make my situation better, but it made it worse. Ghandia tried to make herself look better by making others look bad. I wasn't interested in that game and refused to play it. I felt frustrated and held back — limited to play in a smaller arena than I thought I deserved. Attorneys were always telling me that they liked my work but that I needed to be "friendlier." I felt like people were betraying me — and sometimes they were. Sometimes it was plain old office politics and competition; sometimes it was racism. But the feelings they evoked were the same: I was a child again, locked in an abusive home. I felt unfairly criticized and judged.

There was no one at work who I felt I could talk to. It wasn't just that I didn't trust anyone; I also recognized that my employers are not responsible for shepherding employees through their emotional journeys. People are expected to arrive at work whole, capable, and functional. Managers and supervisors, of course, often suffered from the same traumas and stresses as the employees, but the office was not the place for talk of personal healing. Everyone trudged along, going through the motions, self-medicating if that's what some needed to get through the day. At Temkin, Wielga & Hardt, one of the attorneys had two large boxes of wine delivered to the office every Monday. I always wondered why she didn't have them delivered to her home. I would sign for the delivery and then carry the boxes into her office, setting them carefully on the floor.

I took a train and then a bus to get home from work. On my way home, I often sat beside people who also had just left their jobs. Already, they reeked of alcohol. The minute they left the office, they began consoling themselves. How odd, I thought. If a person doesn't have a criminal record, they aren't examined, interviewed, or questioned for emotional stability. If they can pass a background check, they are assumed to be stable. They limp along, sick and miserable, making other people sick and miserable in the process. The flip side of that was, if a person has a criminal record, they're rejected summarily. They aren't examined, interviewed, or questioned about their state of mind. Their crimes may be twenty-five years old, part of a distant life. Instead, they are presumed unsafe and unstable and are rejected for jobs and opportunities for which they are qualified. This was especially true for white-collar, non-entry-level jobs. I had stayed in touch with a few of my fellow inmates. When anyone we all knew got paroled, one of them would let me know. Most of them were having trouble finding jobs and had signed up with nonprofits, hoping for help. A few had found a neighborhood job like working at the dry cleaners or at the grocery store. But none of them had found the kind of work they were hoping for when they took all those college classes in prison. Most, especially the ones who had been convicted of a violent crime, felt lucky to get anything at all, which is what the nonprofits they turned to for help told them was all they could expect. Employers largely ignored efforts by ex-cons to educate and improve themselves, despite the fact some of them could be the most self-aware people in the room.

I, on the other hand, still had much work to do in the self-awareness department. My psychological balance was precarious. I struggled with workplace stress; I couldn't afford to make a wrong move and lose my job. And it wasn't just at work where I was experiencing a disconnect between who I was and who I thought I could be.

Deciding to make myself a priority in my own life, I hired a personal trainer to help me get into better physical shape. I gained a lot of weight during my marriage, and at my heaviest I was 220 pounds. I had lost a lot of it since my divorce, but I was flabby. I had a free consultation with a female trainer who subsequently referred me to a young man named Joshua Garcia. I hired Josh to train me three times a week — Mondays, Wednesdays, and Fridays — after I got off work. Josh was a knowledgeable, patient, and affordable trainer. After months of training, I was in the best shape of my life. I actually developed a six-pack. I looked good and felt terrific. Unfortunately, I projected the good feelings I was having onto him. I didn't know that women commonly develop romantic feelings for their personal trainers. Exercising generates endorphins, which make a person feel good. Because the woman feels good when she's around her personal trainer, she associates feeling good with the person, rather than with the exercise. I developed a crush on Josh. I kept trying to engage him in conversations in which he would tell me more about his life. He was friendly but somewhat remote. I interpreted this as his "hiding" something from me. In reality, he was probably just being professional. After a year of working out with him, I was frustrated with my inability to break through this barrier. One afternoon, while I was still at work, I sent him an email accusing him of not being honest with me. He responded by telling me that he had shared what he chose to share.

I didn't know how to respect other people's boundaries. No one had respected mine, not as a child, where even my body was constantly violated, and not as an adult, where I stayed in emotionally abusive relationships and justified what the person was doing to me, identifying with them. I had no boundaries, and I didn't recognize them in others. I didn't know where they began or ended. I tended to merge with other people to feel connected. I always lost myself in any relationship. When other people maintained what were, in fact, normal boundaries, I felt threatened and would lash out at them for not being "honest" with me. Unfortunately, the way I lashed out was cruel, but I didn't realize it at the time. I had been treated so cruelly all my life by people who told me that they were being "truthful" that I didn't know how to express my feelings with kindness. I also didn't know how to take responsibility for my own feelings. And I didn't realize that my efforts to get people, Josh in particular, to be "honest" with me and "tell me everything" were an attempt to control them. I needed to be — or at least feel — in control to feel safe. When I felt like people were keeping me out, I felt rejected. And feeling rejected made me feel like the person might do something bad to me.

Josh refused to work out with me after that, and despite my texts and emails, he never spoke to me again.

In every area of my life, I felt like I was walking a tightrope stretched high above a deep abyss. I was chronically unsatisfied. I came across as bitter and cold when I really didn't see myself that way. I felt like I was a nice person inside. And I didn't dislike people. I just didn't feel safe around them.

At the end of my two-year lease at Parliament Apartments, I

decided that I wanted a bigger place. I didn't actually need more space, but for some reason I felt squeezed. I also wanted a quieter location within the complex. In my one-bedroom apartment, I could hear the constant roar of traffic from the nearby expressway — even with my windows closed. I learned what it really meant to be, as their website described, "conveniently located at the intersection of I-25 and I-225."

A move posed a potential problem. I would be treated as a new tenant in a new unit. That meant submitting to a new background check. I was using my maiden name on everything now. I wanted everything I had, including my apartment, to be in the name of Lisa Forbes. I was rebuilding my life under my own name, and doing a pretty good job of it, I thought. At my insistence, the management office ran the background check on Lisa Forbes. My first-degree murder conviction popped up.

I was sitting at my desk at work when I got a call from the apartment manager.

"We need to talk," she said.

I thought maybe my credit score had dropped.

"Okay. What's going on?"

"Well, something came up on your background check."

My heart dropped.

"What is it?" I asked, as if I didn't know.

"Well, it says you've been in prison for murder."

I was at work. I couldn't afford to let anyone overhear me talking about this on the phone.

Quietly, I reminded her that I had been renting at Parliament for two and a half years. They ran a background check when I first applied, and I had passed it.

"Yeah, but that was under a different name," she said.

My heart started to race. I was on the verge of panic.

But I thought I saw a way out — or at least a way to buy some time. She told me that the background check said that I had been in the Illinois Department of Corrections through 2003. I knew that date was a reference to my discharge from parole. It was when I got "off paper," rather than when I was physically released from the prison. I thought I could use this to raise doubt that it was me, obfuscate, get by on a technicality.

"That's impossible," I said. "I can prove where I was when the background check says I was in prison in Illinois. I was living in Georgia. I was working in Georgia. I bought a house in Georgia in 2001. I have references from my job in Georgia. And later I was drawing unemployment benefits from Georgia. So, I couldn't have been in prison in Illinois. The report must be for another person with the same name in Illinois."

She wasn't convinced.

"Well, unless you can prove that there's been some mistake, there's no way I can approve your application with the information that I have here."

I told her that I would need some time to look at the report.

Hoping that everything would work out, I decided to pay that month's rent on my one-bedroom apartment, which I was now leasing month-to-month.

On Friday, May 3, 2013, I went to the drop box outside the leasing office at Parliament and left a check for the full amount due for May. When I went to the office the next day, Saturday morning, to confirm that they had received my check, the manager handed it back to me and said that she could not accept it unless I was able to prove that I was not the person connected with the crime on my background report. My crime was twenty-seven years old. I had been out of prison for thirteen years. I reminded her again that I had a full-time job with excellent references, I already lived in the complex, and I had paid my rent on time for two and a half years. I had never had a problem with either a neighbor or the management.

She did not care.

"We will be in touch with you to get this situation resolved," she said.

I didn't know exactly what that meant, and I was too scared to ask.

I walked back to my apartment, lost in thought about how I was going to get out of this situation. Thirty minutes later there was a knock on my door.

"Who is it?" I asked.

"Maintenance," a man said.

I hadn't put in a service request. When I opened the door, the building's maintenance man, who recognized me from previous times that I had been home while he was in my apartment, handed me a single sheet of paper. Then he looked down, turned, and walked away quickly. Wondering what it could be, I stood in the open door and read the piece of paper. He had just handed me an eviction notice. I had seventy-two hours to get off the premises.

I put the notice on the futon in the living room and went for a long walk to nowhere in particular. I needed to think. I had no idea what I was going to do. I had nowhere to go. I thought about going back to Housing Helpers, but I had only seventy-two hours to move. I didn't think they could help me that quickly. And there was no reason to believe that other places wouldn't run a background check on me, too. I had proudly decided to be Lisa Forbes again. Now I felt like I had shot myself in the foot.

I didn't have resources. There was no one with whom I could simply move in and live. I had furniture and pictures and books and pots and pans and dishes that also needed a new home, but I decided to focus solely on rehoming myself. In a single day, I had gone from feeling like I was rebuilding my life to feeling like I was right back where I'd been the day I walked out of prison, and also the day I walked away from my home in Georgia.

I had been a good tenant. I lived a quiet life. I paid my rent on time and minded my own business. My possessions were a symbol of my progress. I had intentionally purchased cast-iron skillets, pots, and pans because they were essentially indestructible — something I would keep and take care of forever. I scooped them up, walked downstairs to the dumpster, and heaved them in. The clanging pots and pans reminded me of my childhood, when my mother had routinely and intentionally taken things I had valued and thrown them in the garbage when she decided "you don't need that." Now I was being forced to do the same thing to myself. I was being forced to treat myself and my belongings the way that others had treated them. Like garbage.

Dimitri had moved to Florida, and I didn't know anyone in the complex who could help move my furniture down three flights of stairs and out to the dumpster. But in my ongoing research into various methods to resolve childhood trauma, I had met a married couple, Karen McKy and Jim Bates, who taught a form of energy psychology called PSYCH-K.

PSYCH-K is a therapeutic modality that uses Western and ancient philosophies and methods in its processes and balances, including muscle testing, affirming techniques, acupressure points, and whole brain movements. Karen traveled a lot, conducting PSYCH-K workshops all over the world. Jim was about twenty-five years older than Karen and stayed home while she traveled. So, when I called Karen and asked if she and Jim could help me move, she told me that she would be out of town, but that Jim would be happy to do it. Jim came to my apartment eager to help, but he was so much older than me that I didn't want to ask him to carry anything heavy. I was just happy to have a ride. I kept what I could fit in the trunk of Jim's car, which were my clothes, my important papers, and my laptop. I threw everything else that I could physically carry into the dumpster. I left my bed and my futon in the apartment.

Jim drove me the short distance to the leasing office. I entered the double doors for the last time. I handed the young woman at the front desk the keys to the apartment and to the mailbox. The manager didn't come out of her office, and her door stayed closed. "Here are the keys to unit 5203," I told her. "I'm leaving now."

"Good luck!" she responded cheerfully.

I had just thrown my new life into the dumpster, like trash.

"Thanks," I said.

And I walked out.

INTOWN SUITES

That was Sunday, May 5, 2013. On Monday, I went to work at the law firm and acted as if nothing unusual had happened.

"Good morning, how was your weekend?" everyone asked.

"Fine. How was yours?" I answered. I was used to hiding my distress, however severe.

I was paying $340 a week to live in a furnished third-floor "queen" studio apartment at the InTown Suites Extended Stay hotel chain location in Aurora. The suite included a kitchenette, television, high-speed Wi-Fi, a laundry on the premises, and weekly housekeeping. The chain boasted its low weekly rates, but my weekly fee amounted to a $1,360 monthly rate. Even with "utilities included," it still cost me more to rent a room at an extended stay hotel than I had been paying to rent a one-bedroom apartment. The suite wasn't much different from my Motel 6 room, but it was much closer to a bus stop. I could walk three blocks and board a bus bound for downtown Denver. I could also walk to restaurants and grocery stores.

After renting an apartment for two and a half years, it was discombobulating for me to be living yet again in a hotel chain. Why was I going in circles? What was I doing wrong? I was a responsible citizen. Every day I got up, dressed in a nice pair of slacks, a button-down shirt, and a blazer and went to work in a law firm. A *law firm*. But I came home to a place that essentially housed transients. I didn't see myself as a vagabond. I had a bachelor's degree. I was a certified paralegal. I worked forty hours a week. I considered myself a professional. But if I wasn't a ne'er-do-well, why was I forced to live like one? I rented a post office box so that

I wouldn't have to use a chain hotel as my address. I wondered what my co-workers would think of my home. When I went to work, I felt like a fraud.

The firm I worked for, Temkin, Wielga & Hardt, changed, too. First, Mark Wielga decided to retire. I began to work with Betsy Temkin, a lawyer with a prickly personality. She went through three different assistants in the two and a half years I worked at the firm. I didn't get along with Betsy, and I didn't want to support her. I took her rude treatment of the staff personally and filed a complaint with the Colorado Civil Rights Division against Temkin, Wielga & Hardt for racial discrimination. I felt like the attorneys catered to Gina, the white legal assistant, making excuses for her every time she made a mistake but invented reasons to complain about me. One time Betsy sent Patti an email telling her that I was late every day. Patti wouldn't have known, since she was semi-retired and only came in on Tuesdays and Thursdays. But when Patti called me into her office to speak with me about being "tardy," I exploded. The truth was, I was very seldom late, and then only when the bus had been late. Still, I started at 8:00 A.M., and everyone else started at 8:30, and the office didn't officially open until 9:00. So even if I did get there a few minutes late, what was the harm? I always made up the time by taking a shorter lunch. Gina could be late on a regular basis, but it was always because of her kids, so that made it okay. At the time, I felt personally discriminated against, and I still believe that was the case. But my response to Betsy's behavior was exacerbated, I'm sure, by my unhealed wounds. Whenever anyone at work — or anywhere else — appeared to favor someone over me, I was immediately thrown back into my childhood, into a world where my mother doted on my siblings and ignored me.

In May 2013, I joined the much larger law firm Kaplan, Kirsch & Rockwell. I thought a new workplace would enable me to carve out a niche and settle down. I passed a background check. I was never sure why I could pass background checks run by employment companies but not housing agencies. The only thing I could think of was that employment agencies were running background checks that only went back seven years. Since I had been home since 1999, perhaps I was passing seven-year checks. Either way, the signal was confusing. I could get a full-time job at a law firm while, for all practical purposes, I was forced to remain homeless.

I lived in a room at the end of the hallway on the third floor, next to the elevator. The vending machines at InTown Suites stood on the first floor. Sometimes I ran into Reginald Merriweather, who owned and restocked the snack and drink machines. He would always greet me and say good morning. One Saturday he gave me some free potato chips while I waited for him to fill the machine. We chatted and he asked me to lunch. I gave him my Tracfone number and told him to call me after he finished restocking the machines.

We went to the deli at the Whole Foods at the Tiffany Plaza Mall in Denver. I enjoyed the afternoon and felt at ease with him. I thought I might date him again. After all, he didn't live in the hotel. He only worked there. He was a businessman.

Frankly, it had been a long time since I had been with a man. I was thirsty. We began having sex. A few months later, he told me he was moving into a new apartment. Do you want to move in with me? he asked. I jumped at the chance, and moved into the Griffis North Metro apartment complex with Reggie and his eleven-year-old son.

While living with Reggie, I began to repair the damage to my credit report done by my ex-husband, Bashir. Bashir had stopped paying the mortgage on our jointly owned Georgia house at some point after I left, and the house went into pre-foreclosure. I joined PrePaid Legal Services in order to get an attorney to write Bashir a letter. The letter forced him into agreeing to allow a short sale of the house before the bank foreclosed, but by then my credit score had tanked. I wanted my creditors to understand what had really happened. I hired Lexington Law, which drafted letters to various creditors on my behalf, including CitiMortgage, the lender on our Georgia house.

Meanwhile, living with Reggie became a nightmare. He was mean and controlling, and he wanted me to compete with his son for attention — a competition I could never win. Because he met me at InTown Suites, he never stopped seeing me as someone he had rescued from the gutter. I was miserable, but I lived with him for a year. My tolerance for misery was ridiculously high. I endured treatment from other people for a year — or a decade — that an emotionally healthy and self-respecting person wouldn't have taken for a day. By the time I decided I simply could no longer live with Reggie and his son, I had become familiar with the leasing agents in the apartment complex where we lived. I learned that they only ran seven-year background checks on their tenants. I applied for my own apartment and was approved. Reggie and I now lived separately in the same complex, but it was so large that we seldom crossed paths. Once again, I had an apartment but no furniture. I slept on the floor, but I didn't care. I was eager to rebuild my life — again. Still, I wondered: Why did I feel like I was going in circles? Every time I turned around, I was starting over.

Moving forward wasn't easy. After refusing my check and tossing me out, the management at Parliament Apartments had charged my account half a dozen fees. Instead of telling me about those forthcoming charges on the last day I stood in their office, they sent a bill to the address of the apartment they had just kicked me out of! I never saw that bill. But I read about it on my credit report.

Having evicted me from my apartment for a crime I had committed nearly thirty years earlier, Parliament Apartments billed me $413.70 for the following:

- $20 to replace 4 drip pans on the stove top
- $10 to clean the fridge and freezer
- $25 to clean the stove and oven
- $100 to remove 1 bed and 1 futon
- $169.16 in back rent, including days after I left
- $25.52 for utilities

The managers had my cell phone number and could have called me at any time. They didn't. Instead, they turned the bill over to a collection agency. My credit score was already in the toilet, thanks to my ex-husband. Thanks to Parliament Apartments, it had gone down the drain.

I wrote the collections agency and requested a "Pay for Delete" agreement, agreeing to pay the full amount I owed Parliament Apartments if they agreed to have it deleted by all three credit agencies. It seemed like the right thing to do, at the time.

Even so, I couldn't get over what had happened to me at Parliament Apartments. The people in the leasing department knew me. I had lived there more than two and a half years. I'd spent time in their offices. I'd gone to tenant events. I had been a model tenant. Yet a background check and a decades-old crime had turned them against me overnight. What threat did I represent? I didn't confront them, but I was curious about their reasoning.

After all, former prisoners — even those who had been convicted of violent crimes — need a place to live once they get out. Even people convicted of murder don't typically serve natural life sentences and so will ultimately return to life on the outside. Did society expect them to remain transient, without real housing, while holding down a job?

This was a conversation America needed to have, I thought. With the experiences that I'd just been through, I felt especially qualified to start it, but I still had some work to do on myself, first.

ZOE

I became impatient with the pace of my self-help healing. I tapped and tapped and tapped, but I didn't want to have to address every single wound from my past before being able to free myself from chronic anger. That would take the rest of my life. I wanted a quicker way to tell my body, *That was then; this is now*.

I wondered: Was there a more effective way to deal with trauma? Zoe Zimmerman thought so. I found her online. According to her website, she used tapping for "fast breakthroughs" for clients suffering from trauma caused by accidents, surgeries, abuse, physical pain — and dysfunctional families. Tapping, she said, takes the "emotional charge out of traumatic and painful memories and experiences."

Born in Bern, Switzerland, Zoe and her family had lived in various places in Germany. She was a certified EFT practitioner, a trauma therapist, a restorative justice facilitator, and a licensed psychotherapist with an office at 75 Manhattan Drive in Boulder. I made an appointment to see her.

I left early from work to take the bus from Denver to Boulder. When I first moved to Colorado, I had considered living in Boulder. Walking down the street in sixty-degree weather while staring up at snowcapped mountains made me feel like I was living in a picture on a postcard. But it was much more expensive than I could afford. Still, it was beautiful. After getting off the bus, I had to walk four blocks to get to Manhattan Plaza Offices, where Zoe had an office on the second floor. As I walked, I let myself appreciate the majesty of the Rocky Mountains.

I had achieved much by going it alone. This would be the first time I worked with a professional EFT practitioner, and I expected great things from her. She did not disappoint me. She was tall and thin, Pilates-fit, with a dark pixie haircut, a long neck, and a wide smile. She asked probing questions. And she uncovered traumatic connections I had missed.

One involved the vicious murder of Rhonda Sanders, the young woman who lived in another public housing project from ours, the notorious Robert Taylor Homes, who had been stabbed in the throat and thrown into an elevator shaft, and for whose children I used to babysit. After her murder, I had difficulty exposing my throat. In beauty salons, when hairdressers would ask me to lean my head back into a shampoo bowl, I would reflexively cover my throat with my hands.

I gagged and coughed when I revisited the murder with Zoe. I felt like I had to belch or vomit, but nothing came up. Zoe never interfered while this was happening. She remained calm and watchful. "What are you feeling?" she asked.

Zoe helped with other memories. I had a real problem remembering parts of my childhood. Big chunks of it had disappeared. As mentioned earlier, my brothers and sisters would say about someone, "You have to remember them. They were at our house all the time!" Often, I recognized their names, but I couldn't remember what they looked like. Their faces were hazy, blurry, with no distinct features. I knew something was wrong. Zoe called it traumatic amnesia. She said my subconscious protected me by blocking painful memories. My mind didn't want to go there. But at this point, I was ready to bring light to those hidden places.

I wrote a poem to my subconscious mind. "I am ready to see the hidden parts of me, and I approve of myself unconditionally. Make the unconscious conscious." I repeated the poem to myself, and painful memories surfaced.

Zoe comforted me. She pointed out my successes, including some I had ignored.

For instance, I was still bothered by the day my mother and sister robbed me of my penny collection. I felt like I had been robbed by a stranger on the street. My mother and sister were robbers. I had thought at the time as a little girl, *These people do not care about me.*

I couldn't have anything of my own. I couldn't protect myself, and I couldn't protect anything I owned. Anybody could do anything they wanted to me, and anybody could take anything they wanted from me. And they did.

Zoe asked me a question. "Do you have a penny jar now?"

Amazingly, I did. I had been saving pennies since I got my apartment. I had a quart-sized candy jar that I kept at Motel 6. It sat on the nightstand in my bedroom. And it was full of pennies. Zoe used that fact to unstick me from those still-raw emotions associated with my mother and sister. I was now in a position where I could have something, anything — even a penny jar — and no one was going to take it from me. I didn't have to continue to feel vulnerable and unsafe.

After six sessions with Zoe, I went back to tapping on my own. But now, I was standing on higher ground.

A ROOM FULL OF FACES

I had two more memories to tackle. The first had to do with murder.

On a cold Chicago day, I had plunged a kitchen knife into James Bankston's chest. I had stabbed him while his new wife, stepchildren, friends, and our two-year-old daughter looked on.

Why did I do it? James had given me a daughter, Mercedes. He had promised to marry me and buy me a ring. Then he married another woman and didn't tell me.

I had endured years of bullying, sexual abuse, and religious ostracism. My heart had taken a terrible beating. But I knew I could never heal myself if I stood over James Bankston's grave and focused solely on *my* pain.

Yet what was I supposed to do now? Tap about a murder?

Undoubtedly, James Bankston died for the sins of others. My anger at the world did not start with James. It started with my family. My mother rejected me long before James did. My brother molested me for years, making me feel powerless and used. James was a stand-in for people he didn't even know. Not that he didn't abuse me, too. I was seventeen when I met him. He was twenty-three. I read Harlequin romance novels and had never dated. He toyed with me, lied to me, and abandoned me. Still, he owned a home and took care of his mother until she died. He shared his home with his sister and was a father figure to his nephew. The truth was, James Bankston was far from a bad person. He was, in many ways, a good man. And there is no way my killing him was justified.

Could I tap that away?

Ultimately, I decided that it wasn't about justifying my crime. It was about understanding it. And making sure I would never react in the same way again.

At my sentencing, the judge had declared: "It is too late for James Bankston. And indeed, it is too late for Lisa Forbes."

But the judge was wrong. I was not a violent person. Michael Jackson's "Thriller" video gave me nightmares. Violence on TV turned my stomach. The jury never heard my story, thanks to my public defender deciding my past life didn't matter. So, the jury was left with a picture of a jealous, unstable woman sent into a rage because her boyfriend had rejected her.

I dove deeply into my emotions. It felt dangerous, tricky. The massive resentment, the profound bitterness, the colossal rage, the feelings of unfairness and injustice — could I handle it? For years, I had rejected my emotions and built walls around myself. I pretended that I didn't have any feelings. If they surfaced, I buried them. I was numb. Moving away had not fixed my life. I had taken my feelings with me and projected their personalities onto strangers.

Still, I knew it wasn't too late for me to confront that terrible day in Chicago. One hot summer day in August 2012, I took the first step. I closed my eyes and asked myself the question the prosecution had asked me when I took the witness stand.

How did it feel to take a butcher knife and plunge it into James Bankston's chest?

When the assistant state's attorney screamed at me in April 1987, I froze, sat there, stared at him, and said nothing, a reflex common among trauma victims. I'm sure the jury interpreted my silence as a lack of remorse and an admission of guilt.

This time — more than twenty-five years later — I responded.

"Even though I killed someone, I deeply and completely love and accept myself, anyway," I said while tapping.

This is crazy, I thought. I felt like throwing up. I went further back in time, to the day of the murder. This time I saw some of the same things I'd always seen — shadowy figures and faces — but I saw them differently or saw things I'd never seen before.

I saw things that had enraged me and things that had thrown me off balance. I felt ridiculed and scorned as James and Yvette spoke lovingly to each other in front of me, calling each other "baby." I sat on the sofa beside him, feeling like an idiot because he had once introduced Yvette to me as his cousin. James smirked, took a sip of tea, and placed the cup on the table.

Shaking his head and laughing, he'd said, "I'm sorry."

His was the same look of disdain, mockery, and utter contempt that I'd seen on my mother's face many times — a look that said, *You are nobody, and nobody cares what you want or why you're here.* I heard the scorn in the voices of my brothers and sisters, too. Suddenly there seemed to me to be a lot of people standing in the hallway. I looked at James and said, "I'm sorry, too."

Tapping, I heard James ask, "What's that?" when I then reached in my bag and pulled out the knife. I saw the shock on his face when he realized what was about to happen. I saw the wince he made when the knife went in. I saw him reach for the cup of hot tea and throw it in my face. I was wearing contact lenses, and for a few seconds, I couldn't see. I ran to the front door, but I couldn't open the locked storm door.

I remembered feeling trapped, banging on the door, trying to get the attention of two men coming out of a house across the street, and screaming for help. I could see them again as they started running toward the house but then fled when a police car pulled up, sirens blaring. I relived hearing for the first time, over the sound of the police sirens, screaming and crying behind me as the people in the house tried to help James, and two police officers ran up the six or seven stairs leading to the front porch and opened the storm door. One of the policemen — they were both white — pulled his gun on me and said, "Don't go anywhere." The other officer went into the house. Then he came out, handcuffed me, and put me into the back seat of the police car.

I watched as the paramedics carried James Bankston on a stretcher and placed him in an ambulance. He was alive. I saw his face. His eyes were closed. I didn't see any blood. I remembered thinking, *He'll be all right.* He died the next day. He'd had surgery, but the doctors couldn't stop the bleeding. I never saw the physical aftermath of what I had done — but his family did. And, for the first time, I let myself go back to that moment and I tried to experience it the way James did. His wife had testified on the witness stand that James had said, "Look what she did to me." I thought about how that moment must have felt to his wife and other family members who were there. I thought about how his wife must have blamed herself for being the one who opened the door and let me in. Accessing and reliving that day from their point of view was the hardest thing I'd ever done.

ARMAGEDDON

But I still had one last thing to face. I couldn't stop thinking about it, even though I desperately wanted to.

On a Saturday afternoon in August 1985, when I was nineteen, I suffered a breakdown while my daughter slept in my bed. I wanted to nap alongside her, but a painful memory would not let go of me.

"That muthafucka *ruined my life!*" I screamed at the four walls of my apartment in Milwaukee, my eyes tightly closed, my hands balled into fists.

The unwanted memory of my brother's sexual advances flooded my mind and triggered a mental meltdown. I saw it clearly. I was eight years old, lying on top of Kirk, feeling his penis get hard, curl up, and move underneath me.

Although Kirk had molested me in many ways over the years, it was that memory — that shameful day when he had pulled me on top of him, and I stayed there, grinding — that relentlessly played over and over in my mind. The actual event had probably lasted less than sixty seconds, but I had experienced the shame of it every day since. It tormented me, made me feel guilty, nasty, and undeserving. It made me feel like I deserved to be molested all those subsequent times over the course of years because I had once joined my brother in the act.

The memory never went away. One day I did the math. My brother had abused me daily, from the time I was eight to the day I turned twelve. If he had only molested me once a day, then I would have endured 1,460 sexual attacks before he stopped. But he didn't attack me *once* a day. Kirk groped me, rubbed me, squeezed me, and masturbated while staring at me four or five times a day.

On cold, rainy, or snowy days, Kirk, stuck in the house, amused himself by groping me every few minutes.

My brother had sexually assaulted me many thousands of times during my childhood.

Grappling with those memories for decades had mentally and psychologically exhausted me.

Treating my anxiety and other lasting effects of my trauma wouldn't be easy. I needed help, but I also accepted that I would have to push myself. I would have to be willing to do the work.

I had lived with the idea of imminent Armageddon all my life, thanks to my mother and her religious fears.

"Then there will be great tribulation such as has not occurred since the world's beginning," she said, quoting from the Bible.

But I no longer had the luxury of even subconsciously worrying about Armageddon.

I was about to fight my own life-and-death struggle.

I could tell that the hardest battle I was ever going to fight was the war between what I *knew* (which was that I wasn't a bad person) and what I *felt* (which was that I must have somehow deserved what had happened to me).

In my mind, I had to go back to Chicago. I had to climb those dark, urine-soaked stairs to the sixth floor of the housing projects where my brother had sexually abused me every day for years.

I had to go home.

After my sessions with Zoe, I made a decision. I would approach Kirk the way I had approached James. I couldn't change the past, but I could change the future. I couldn't change what I had done, or what Kirk had done, but I could decide not to let the pain turn me into somebody I didn't want to be.

LISA FORBES INC.

I rarely remembered my dreams during the ten years I lived with Bashir. One night after I left him and moved to Colorado, I dreamed about our house in Georgia. I pulled into the driveway in our silver-colored Honda Accord. I got out of the car, and in the right corner of the garage, I saw a snake eating a lizard from the tail end. I looked at it and went into the house. In my dream, I spent the afternoon running errands. Each time I shopped, I brought my purchases into the house through the garage. I always stopped to observe the snake's progress.

The lizard was alive, but it was not fighting. Each time I checked, the snake had swallowed a little more of the lizard. Eventually, the snake swallowed all but the lizard's face. The lizard still had its eyes open. In the dream I realized that the lizard was allowing itself to be consumed. Then I woke up.

I interpreted the dream to mean I had been the lizard, and I had allowed myself to be consumed.

In 2015, I launched Lisa Forbes Inc. as a consulting firm for restored citizens and the businesses that wanted to hire them. I envisioned being a liaison between the two. I hired Risha Grant LLC, a Black-owned, woman-owned business in Tulsa, Oklahoma, to design my brochures and website. I paid $6,000 for the services (including a photoshoot and marketing).

Juggling running my start-up with keeping my full-time job as a paralegal at a law firm was a challenge. I felt like two different people living in two different worlds. On the one hand, I worked as a support staffer for somebody else. On the other hand, I was a businesswoman who needed her own support staff.

I had spent years working with nonprofit organizations claiming to help parolees find jobs and stay out of jail. Most didn't. The agencies lived on grant money. They said all the right things to get funding. Then they ran the same programs that had never really worked.

I had a radical approach to reentry for people whom society at large tends to refer to as ex-cons, but whom I call restored citizens. First, I believed that a prisoner's street skills could benefit the business world. The skills required to be a success at selling illegal drugs were similar to those required to develop and market legal goods. Of course, restored citizens couldn't make that point on a résumé. For them, producing a résumé was a demoralizing and difficult exercise, one that reinforced their belief that they could never make it in the workforce.

Second, I concluded that nonprofits were too busy scrambling for funds to help. They perpetuated social problems through patronizing services. Worse, many of their executives had little or no personal experience in overcoming the challenges their clients faced — yet they represented themselves as authorities on those very challenges.

There must be a better way, I thought.

The former prisoners I knew were struggling to make it on the outside world — and the odds were against them. According to the US Sentencing Commission, roughly half of the offenders released from prison or placed on probation are rearrested within eight years. Some committed new crimes; others were in some technical violation of a condition of their probation or release.

Why did so many former inmates return to prison?

It wasn't because it was hard for them to find work or a place to live, although that was certainly a factor. A background check could stop them from getting a job or an apartment. I had lived in motel rooms; I had been thrown out of an apartment complex after living there for years when the manager discovered my ex-felon status; and I had worked at temporary low-paying jobs because that was the only work people would hire me for, regardless of my abilities and qualifications.

But so many former prisoners suffered from the same thing I did: trauma. Like me, they were caught in a terrible loop that included the same bad decisions they had made before. Even when they got jobs, they lost them. Some, after they got an apartment, couldn't keep it. When I talked to former prisoners, I heard the trauma in their voices. I saw disturbance and trauma when I looked into their eyes.

A woman charged with stealing clothes tried to build a new life. She got a job at a fast-food restaurant and rented a one-bedroom apartment. When she sought to regain custody of her children — placed in foster care while she was in prison — she was told she would need a three-bedroom apartment as a condition for getting her own children back. Her young girls would need to have their own bedroom, as would her thirteen-year-old son. None of them were allowed to share a room with her. The woman fell into despair. She could barely afford a one-bedroom apartment. How could she pay for a bigger home? She couldn't get a better job because she kept failing background checks, even though she had served her time and "paid her debt to society." So, she kept her fast-food job and sold stolen goods on the side. Soon, she was back in prison, and her children were back in foster care.

Restored citizens need more than job placement. They need to be placed in better jobs. They need to be able to enter the workforce at the levels of which they are actually capable. Why should we be relegated to only the most entry-level and lowest-paying jobs, when we earned college degrees and learned trades while incarcerated?

And restored citizens need help to deal with post-traumatic stress disorder, a burden exacerbated by their post-prison challenges. They don't need just criminal justice reform. They need a personal revolution, and they need support and knowledge to help them achieve it.

The truth is, criminal justice/prison reform as it is currently being proposed would not have helped me at all. Like most people in prison, my problems started well before I ever got there.

There is no such thing as an isolated problem. I believe personal reform, family reform, community reform, and social reform cannot be separated from prison reform and criminal justice reform.

Merely opening the prison doors and sending traumatized people back to their traumatized families living in their traumatized communities is not the answer. Violent behavior is often the direct result of early childhood trauma. The commission of a violent offense is not irrefutable evidence of the offender possessing a violent nature. Many violent offenders are not inherently violent people, and they should not be ignored in society's quest to rehabilitate our citizens, our workforce, and our national economy.

For me, a feeling of helplessness and the loss of power and control was central to my experience of trauma — as were involuntary and frequent ruminations about past events and responding as if they were occurring in the present. The goal I set for myself, therefore, was to find a way to create a sense of personal safety and personal empowerment — as opposed to constantly feeling that I was at the mercy of others and that my present reality was an inescapable product of my trauma and disadvantages.

The only solution to the social problems we face, the only way for us not to be still discussing them a generation from now, is to accept that a permanent solution to any problem requires some degree of personal responsibility for change. Unless you are completely incapable of doing so, you have to help me help you. There's no magic wand that anyone can wave over you and change everything in your circumstances while you do nothing different. What I just wrote is usually considered politically incorrect because people tend to conflate it with "blaming the victim." But I'm suggesting no such thing. Personal responsibility is the only enduring path to a "normal life." That's a hard fact. The saying "If you keep doing what you've been doing you'll keep getting what you've been getting" is cliché, but nevertheless true.

To realize a life of fulfillment and contentment, I first had to admit that, like most former prisoners I knew who were struggling to attain a "normal life," I had been experiencing and complaining about the same problems for decades. We had all suffered hardships and unwanted situations. Even though we were all claiming to want change, we were not achieving resolution. I realized that we weren't bad people. We were simply people whose external circumstances and internal mental patterns kept reinforcing each other.

There is no such thing as building a better world without improving individuals. For me, the process was not pretty, simple, or linear. But it was effective, and it was worth it.

Lisa Forbes Inc., I decided, would not focus on prison reform. Criminal justice reform is a noble cause, but the circumstances that led me to spend fourteen years behind prison walls would not have been affected by criminal justice reform. Moreover, even though I read hundreds of books during my fourteen years behind bars, none of them gave me awareness, let alone understanding, of the trauma I was dealing with.

Untreated trauma is a major link in the chain of recidivism.

The mission of Lisa Forbes Inc. would be to empower restored citizens and get them to the point where they could turn to a counselor and say, "Thank you for your help; I can take it from here."

I would be its first client.

book four

The Way Forward

FROM INVISIBLE TO RESTORED

I belong to an American family some call invisible.

The fact is, we're everywhere. In 2016, the year after I started Lisa Forbes Inc., an estimated 110 million Americans had an arrest record — more than twice as many people as in 1997. Today, the American criminal justice system holds nearly 2.3 million people in more than seven thousand state and federal prisons, juvenile correctional facilities, local jails, and immigration detention facilities. The recidivism rate hovers between 65 and 75 percent.

The day that I walked out of Dixon Correctional Center in Dixon, Illinois, I began to think of myself not as an ex-con or a former felon but as a restored citizen. Later, when I moved to Georgia, I didn't define myself as the person who killed a man on a cold December day in Chicago. I wasn't the person who tried to scale a prison fence. And when I moved to Colorado, I wasn't the person who left my husband back in Georgia after our marriage fell apart.

I was a single Black woman, an American citizen, starting a new life in a new job in a new state.

I knew it was an important distinction. How I referred to myself mattered. The label *ex-con*, I knew, would only hamper me — just as it hinders millions of other restored citizens. It keeps them focused on the past, which is the last place most of them need to be. Identity is destiny.

If I'm an ex-convict, I'm an outsider.

If I'm a restored citizen, I have the same rights as any other citizen — and I have the same responsibilities.

After leaving the Illinois prison system, I registered to vote. In the first election to come along, I found a nearby polling place and

made a mark on a ballot. My first vote was for a state representative. I felt proud that day. I wanted not only to regain but also to
exercise every freedom I had lost. I got a passport even though I
wasn't allowed to travel yet.

I was reclaiming my identity. Jehovah's Witnesses don't vote. So,
in addition to claiming a lost American right, I was also forging a
new self, separate from my parents and their beliefs. I didn't stop
there. I joined the League of Women Voters, helped organize
candidate forums and debates and edited *The Voter*, the monthly
newsletter for my local county league.

I was lucky. According to a recent study by the Sentencing
Project, an estimated six million Americans are forbidden to vote
because of felony disenfranchisement. Some states won't allow
prisoners to vote while they are on probation or parole. Some can
permanently disenfranchise felons convicted of certain crimes.

This issue is crucially important. Restored citizens need a voice
in who runs their government, because the people in government
make decisions that affect prisoners and former prisoners. Most
people — including elected officials — don't realize that the
distinction between "nonviolent" offenders and "violent" offenders is critically flawed. Here's the reality: Some people jailed for
nonviolent offenses are violent people who were arrested on a
nonviolent offense. And a lot of people serving prison time for
violent crimes are fundamentally nonviolent people who simply
did something crazy during a psychological breakdown. This is
particularly true of women in prison. It was certainly true of me.

And yet, even politicians who claim that the issues of mass incarceration, recidivism, and structural racism are important to them
don't get it. During the last presidential election, former Texas
congressman Beto O'Rourke, who was running for the 2020
Democratic nomination, suggested that he might rethink disenfranchisement for "nonviolent offenders" but not for "violent
criminals." I thought it was interesting that he distinguished

between "offenders" (nonviolent) and "criminals" (violent). One of his rivals for the nomination, Kamala Harris, formerly California's attorney general, stated that "people who commit murder . . . should be deprived of their rights." Even progressive Massachusetts senator Elizabeth Warren said she's "not there yet."

Voting is one way to reenter society and feel invested in it, a reason to not live and behave like an outsider.

Through Lisa Forbes Inc., however, I hoped to do more than advocate for this single issue, as important as it may be. Former prisoners face challenges at every turn. They must earn a living, find a place to live, repair family divisions, get healthy, and make new friends — all while meeting the demands of their parole.

I faced all of those challenges. As a restored citizen, I struggled to find a steady job despite having a paralegal certificate and a bachelor's degree in business administration. I worked temporary gigs — jobs that lasted from a few days to a few weeks — and struggled to pay the rent and eat. I knew a background check could cost me a job — a job I was qualified to do — and force me into homelessness.

Living on temp work was stressful. It paid $10 to $12 an hour — and did not include health insurance or paid sick days. I couldn't afford to lose a day. If I did, I'd miss a rent payment, something I never did. Even on days I didn't feel well, I boarded a bus and headed to the office.

I always hoped that one of the jobs would become permanent. None did. If an agency had no work, I tried other places. Every time I signed with each new agency, I had to take the same tests, even though I had worked at various law offices. Over and over, I had to prove that I could read, spell, and type.

There were weeks at a time when I ate by ordering from the dollar menu at fast-food restaurants. Eating healthy wasn't an option, and I suffered from it. Poor diets, researchers say, play a role in worsening mood disorders, such as anxiety and depression.

Many restored citizens feed not only themselves but also their children a daily diet of cheap fast food.

At Lisa Forbes Inc., I wanted to act as a mediator between America's restored citizens and the business world. I was inspired, in part, by the 1981 business book *Getting to Yes* by Roger Fisher and William Ury. The authors emphasize several principles of negotiation. Focus on interests, not positions. Seek solutions that benefit both sides.

Perception is a big problem. Business owners worry that former prisoners will be risky hires. And restored citizens worry they aren't wanted. The media often make matters worse, too often pandering to our fears, anger, distrust, and anxiety. Real issues cannot be addressed when emotions, and sensationalism, run the show.

My question to employers and to their employees is this: Why do you think you can't work with restored citizens? You live with their relatives and loved ones in your neighborhood. They shop in your superstores and walk among you on the streets. You sit next to them on the train or stand in line behind them at the grocery store. They're at the table next to you in the restaurant.

My question to landlords and their current tenants is this: Why are you reluctant to rent an apartment to or live next door to a restored citizen? Do you realize their spouses or other family members can just leave their names off the rental application and lease, and so all you are doing is driving them deeper into the shadows and deluding yourselves?

Our society's entire approach, making it so difficult for restored citizens to secure decent jobs and housing, is irrational. It is in everyone's best interests for restored citizens to feel less desperate about securing life's basic necessities.

Integrating restored citizens into the workforce can be done without compromising public safety.

Some people with criminal records have no intention or desire to fit into anyone's system — in the workforce or anywhere else.

But that's a small subset of a group of people who need help and support.

Of course, employers must be careful. No one is suggesting, for instance, that a restored citizen with a history of child abuse should work with children. But people are denied work when there is no connection between their new job and the crime they were convicted of committing months or years or even decades ago. This treatment amounts to a kind of perpetual punishment for a debt that has been paid in full.

Businesses and organizations need help understanding the restored citizen population. And undoubtedly many restored citizens, once they get the fundamental trauma and other mental health help they will need to get to the point of "I Can Take It from Here" will still need to acquire marketable skills, coaching on how to apply for work, and more.

As someone with a foot in both worlds, I knew I could help. I knew I could articulate not just the problems but also the solutions.

I knew I could ask the hard questions:

What are our mutual interests?

And what is at stake if we don't succeed?

Are the revered values of American resilience and self-reliance — picking oneself up, dusting oneself off, and starting over — applicable to restored citizens?

The answer is yes.

There's another justification for training and hiring restored citizens: When people can't find a job that pays a living wage, they often commit crimes such as petty theft simply to make ends meet — and end up in jail again. And that affects everyone: the business owners from whom they steal, their own families and children, and every American taxpayer who has to pay for a costly prison system that doesn't actually make them any safer.

Every one of us has a stake in this issue.

When I say practically anyone can construct a dignified existence out of the smoldering ruins of a damaged life, it's not theory to me. I'm speaking from personal experience.

Sexual abuse, bullying, religious abuse, living in public housing projects, single teenage parenthood, incarceration, eviction, unemployment, underemployment, living on welfare, job stress, working two jobs just trying to make it, divorce, homelessness, physical health problems, domestic violence, depression, suicidal thoughts, PTSD — you name it, I've been there.

Rather than feeling helpless and hopeless, I drew a different conclusion about my life. I wrote editorials, read manifestos, and met with a documentary filmmaker while in prison, trying to be seen as a human being and not just a criminal — an "inmate" convicted of a violent crime. I didn't want the government or a politician to define me. Any politician who convinces you that your ability to live the life you choose depends solely on what the government is doing, or is not doing, is preying on your sense of inferiority. As former First Lady Eleanor Roosevelt said, "No one can make you feel inferior without your consent."

That's not to say that people we elect as our leaders have no responsibility to restored citizens. The government doesn't owe us a living, but it does have an obligation to safeguard structures that allow us the opportunity to create our own successful lives, not punitive and wrongheaded rules and laws that prevent us from doing so.

I wanted Lisa Forbes Inc. ("LFI") to be distinct from the "reentry programs" that promote perpetual dependency or limit restored citizens to the minimum-wage jobs that make it impossible for a working person to afford an apartment. Many restored citizens are among the "working homeless."

But even while I urge government to play its role in a more intelligent way, my message to restored citizens is this: You don't have to depend forever on nonprofits, charities, and the government to succeed. You have the power to create a better life for yourself.

Why, then, do so many feel they have no power? Why are so many discouraged? During my research, I came across the term *shifting baseline syndrome*, which has to do with the difficulty of monitoring and registering gradual change. Although researchers first used the term to describe our perceptions of gradual changes in the environment, psychologists and others have applied it to other fields.

For example, each generation defines *natural* or *normal* according to current conditions and personal experiences. With each new generation, expectations shift. Changes are so incremental that they're hard to spot, but they have a cumulative effect over time. The end result is that we lower our standards without even realizing it.

Black Americans, for a variety of historical reasons, have suffered from the practical effects of the shifting baseline phenomenon.

They say that history repeats itself. There's a specific part of history that we need to repeat.

Many people — most importantly Black people — don't realize the significant participation of Black Americans in governance at all levels during Reconstruction, right after the Civil War, from 1865 to 1877.

One of the most important aspects of Reconstruction was the active participation of Black people (including thousands of formerly enslaved people) in the political, economic, and social life of the South. The era was to a great extent defined by their quest not just for equality but for *autonomy*, both as individuals and for the Black community as a whole. They organized Equal Rights Leagues throughout the South and held state and local conventions. Sixteen African Americans served in the US Congress during Reconstruction. Voters elected six hundred Black candidates to the state legislatures. Hundreds more held local offices across the South. In all, some two thousand African Americans held public office, from the local level all the way up to the US Senate.

And while there has been much progress in many areas since the 1800s, in some critical ways — for example, in education — we have allowed our expectations to decline monstrously. Margot Lee Shetterly, the author of the book *Hidden Figures: The American Dream and the Untold Story of the Black Women Mathematicians Who Helped Win the Space Race*, wrote, "As a child, I knew so many African Americans working in science, math, and engineering that I thought that's just what black folks did." So how did we get to the point in 2022 where "black folks" graduating from high school without being able to read or do basic math is accepted as just another of America's perpetual social problems? Why do we think this is just how "black folks" are?

We know that Black Americans have been hit especially hard by the court and prison system. According to a Pew Research study, Blacks in 2018 represented 33 percent of the sentenced prison population, nearly triple their 12 percent share of the US adult population. But how are we approaching dealing with those statistics? Do we need "reform" by other people, or do we need self-sufficiency — *autonomy* — as Black people understood we did during Reconstruction?

All of these things — voting rights, housing, a decent job, education, changes in how we define restored citizens — are key to helping restored citizens succeed after prison.

But none of it matters in the long term if we don't tackle the root cause of many crimes: trauma. Untreated trauma is also at the root of most restored citizens' continuing problems after they have served their sentences. They may have job skills but lack emotional stability. If they lose a job, they lose their home or apartment and risk losing custody of their children. It's a domino effect.

These restored citizens — and sometimes, their teenage or older children — are often caught in the revolving door of ineffective social programs.

When social programs tell people they just "need a job" or "affordable housing," they fail to get to the heart of the problem.

We can do better.

The psychiatrist, trauma research author, and educator Bessel van der Kolk has studied post-traumatic stress since the 1970s. You don't have to be a soldier to experience PTSD, he argues in his landmark book, *The Body Keeps the Score*. "Trauma happens to us, our friends, our families, and our neighbors."

The good news? The brain can form and reorganize synaptic connections in response to trauma to help survivors "feel fully alive in the present and move on with their lives."

According to Kolk, there are several ways to change behavior: talking and reconnecting with others while processing the memories of the trauma; taking medicines that shut down inappropriate alarm reactions; using technologies that change the way the brain organizes information; and allowing the body to have experiences that deeply and viscerally contradict the helplessness, rage, or collapse that result from trauma. Most people require a combination of approaches.

A combination was required for me, too. I found people like Karen McKy and Jim Bates to talk with while processing the memories of the trauma with PSYCH-K processes. But tapping was a huge part of my recovery, and a method that will also help many other traumatized people.

The children of prisoners and restored citizens suffer, too. My daughter continues to deal with abandonment issues brought on by my sudden disappearance from her life at the age of two. She's an adult now, but a part of her still feels unwanted by me. With her conscious mind, she says, "I love you, and I know you love me." Subconsciously, she feels rejected. She struggles with issues created by my absence. Raised by her grandparents, she always felt like she was in the way. She felt she had stifled their plans for their senior

years because they had to focus, instead, on raising her. They were
in their sixties and raising a toddler. She was two years old when I
was arrested and "sixteen going on thirty" when I came home.

On top of that, she had to deal with the fact that I killed her
father. She treasures the Cabbage Patch doll James gave her as a
child, and she keeps the single picture that I ever had of James —
one in which he is holding her when she was a year old. Where
were her loyalties supposed to lie? The breach in our connection
was real, and it was deep. Not only are restored prisoners traumatized, but their children are also often traumatized by their absence.
Our sudden release seldom does little to remove that pain. And the
children of restored citizens — many of whom suffer from depression, learning disabilities, anxiety, developmental delays, and other
issues — are more likely to go to jail, too.

My daughter has so far escaped that fate, but she is by no means
unscathed. And restored citizens who attempt to re-create a relationship with their children — who often are no longer "children"
by the time the parent is released — have to deal with the guilt they
frequently feel when they see their sons and daughters struggling
with emotional problems that their own incarceration may have
caused or, at the very least, contributed to. My daughter was in the
room when I stabbed James. Although she was only two years old
at the time, she has angrily confronted me as an adult with accusa-
tions of me being a hateful person because of "my behavior."
Referring to James's murder, she asked me, "Don't you think you
should have protected me from seeing that?" — even though she
has no conscious memory of actually seeing me do anything.

How do I and others like me deal with that kind of trauma-filled
resentment from our children while still healing from our own
personal trauma?

We also need to recognize that many people in prison have been
victims of sex crimes. Those crimes aren't limited to rape.

Forcible touching often occurs at home. In such cases, the attacker is usually a relative of the victim. My older brother squeezed, groped, grabbed, and bumped and grinded on me for years. In New York, forcible touching is considered a sex crime; the names of people convicted of forcible touching appear on the state's sex offender registry.

By this standard I should be considered not just the perpetrator of a crime but also the victim of one. The judge for my case didn't consider the years of criminal sexual abuse I had endured when he sentenced me for the crime I committed. Many judges, juries, and prosecutors don't. But there are legal precedents allowing for leniency for defendants who commit crimes following a history of childhood abuse.

The Mayo Clinic explains it this way:

> If you have a mental health problem called "dissociation," your sense of disconnect from the world around you is often complicated. Dissociation is a break in how your mind handles information. You may feel disconnected from your thoughts, feelings, memories, and surroundings. It can affect your sense of identity and your perception of time. The symptoms often go away on their own. You may need treatment, though, if your dissociation is happening because you've had an extremely troubling experience. When you have dissociation, you may forget things or have gaps in your memory. You may notice other changes in the way you feel, such as feel emotionally numb or detached, feel little or no pain, have intense flashbacks that feel real, not remember how you got somewhere, or get absorbed in a fantasy world that seems real.

What drives dissociation? Trauma.

> You may psychologically disconnect from the present
> moment if something really bad happens to you. This is
> called Peritraumatic Dissociation. Experts believe this
> is a technique your mind uses to protect you from the
> full impact of the upsetting experience you had.
> Peritraumatic dissociation can happen as a result of
> sexual or physical assault, childhood abuse, combat,
> motor vehicle accidents, and natural disasters.

I suffer from almost everything on the Mayo Clinic's list. I may
not have gone to war, but many consider Chicago's public housing
a war zone. According to one scholar, the Chicago Housing
Authority "created a system that concentrated low-income African
American families in chaotic, disorganized, and very often violent
communities."

Against that backdrop, I did my best to survive. It wasn't easy.
My drunken father screamed and cursed and randomly slapped us
on the backs of our heads whenever we walked past him. My
brother molested me. My sisters bullied me. And my mother? She
alternated between ignoring me and laughing at me while she
talked endlessly about the imminent end of the world.

What happens to someone who lives in that environment? What
happens to a child who is forming their identity while immersed
in those conditions? They very often experience dissociation,
post-traumatic stress disorder, and acute stress disorder.

Children with such disorders may stare out the window a lot (as
I did); have imaginary friends (as I did); seem spacey (as I did);
and forget they've said or done something (as I did). They may
escape reality in involuntary and unhealthy ways as they fight to
keep difficult memories at bay (as I did, fleeing into Harlequin
romance novels even as a preteen).

Mental health experts divide dissociative disorders into three groups. The first — according to the *Diagnostic and Statistical Manual of Mental Disorders*, published by the American Psychiatric Association — is dissociative amnesia. Those who suffer from it can't recall events and people in their lives, especially those from a traumatic time. I'm in that group. Sometimes one of my sisters will mention someone from our past, and I'll stare and ask, "Who?" "How can you not remember so-and-so?" they'll ask. Sometimes I can conjure up a fuzzy recollection of the person, but usually I can't.

Another type of disorder is depersonalization-derealization disorder. People with this disorder experience an ongoing or episodic sense of detachment. They're disconnected. They observe their actions, feelings, and thoughts from a distance, as though they're watching a movie. I felt that way during my trial. "You look like everything is just washing over you," my sister Net told me during a jury break. "It's like you're here, but you're not here." I also felt that way when I was being shipped from the county jail to the state prison. Other people around you may seem foggy or dream-like when you're experiencing this disorder — like the ghostly figures I saw in James's house the day I stabbed him.

There's also dissociative identity disorder, formerly known as multiple personality disorder. As early as the 1880s, some courts have accepted "irresistible impulse" as a legal defense. The argument goes like this: If a defendant suffers from a disease or unsoundness of mind and acts on an impulse that they cannot control, they are not fully accountable for their actions.

I believe that's why I didn't leave James's house when I knocked and nobody answered. People ask, "Why didn't you just go elsewhere until your parents came home?" I don't know the answer to that question. That house pulled me in. I had an irresistible impulse to get inside and be reassured by James that everything was okay. I can't explain it, so in retrospect, I can understand why a jury couldn't understand it.

And therein lies the problem: We must begin to understand this crisis and call it what it is.

We as a society are facing an emotional trauma plague — a plague that has been misdiagnosed as an economic problem. The violent crime rate in our country is a mental health emergency.

We must do something different.

The people helping restored citizens — social workers and experts — need to do something they've never done before. They need to ask different questions and they need to ask them of other people. I've been to a lot of conferences on how to "help ex-offenders," and almost none of them included a restored citizen on the panel as an expert. Instead, they relied on "ex-offenders" to provide emotionally charged testimony about much they've been "helped" by the organization.

These types of programs will never create permanent change for the millions of restored citizens coping with trauma.

Some believe success includes abolishing the nation's prison system by ending classism, racism, and capitalism, "the driving forces behind our criminal justice system." If a person has to wait for these game-changing things to happen before they can be successful, they might as well forget it. It's unlikely to occur in their lifetime.

Time is not on our side.

Mass incarceration has led to overcrowded prisons and strained state budgets. According to the Bureau of Justice Statistics, the United States spends more than $80 billion each year to keep more than two million people behind bars.

According to the Pew Research Center, the number of prison and jail inmates in the US has decreased in recent years. But that doesn't mean that the people who have been released are employed, healthy, and self-sufficient taxpayers. It doesn't mean that these untreated restored citizens are not being retraumatized by problems in their families and violence in their communities. It doesn't mean they won't return to prison.

What is the answer?

We need a multipronged strategy.

Various bills have been introduced on the state and federal levels to create an "Office of New Americans" to help immigrants integrate into the social, cultural, economic, and civic life of the United States. My current home state, Colorado, has such a bill pending.

I say we need a similar bill for restored citizens.

A National Office of Restored Americans Act would help restored citizens ease into the social, cultural, economic, and civic life of the United States. Like the bills for immigrants, it would tackle issues such as language learning, adult education, workforce training, health care, and other issues. And it would address trauma.

The Colorado Office of New Americans states: "The work we do as a community-based organization to help immigrants navigate systems, find employment, become self-sufficient, and integrate into their new community does not happen in isolation."

Laudable goals. Restored citizens need the same kind of help — not a job that pays so little that they qualify for government assistance. Becoming a successful citizen "does not happen in isolation" for new citizens (immigrants) or for restored citizens. They both need community support. But ex-prisoners need more. They can't become "self-sufficient" if someone running a background check can discover a decades-old conviction and ruin their lives.

Emphasizing trauma resolution in the training and support offered to restored citizens will help, too. Many restored citizens may be free from prison but are dragging their troubled past behind them. These invisible chains weigh them down in ways more lasting and debilitating than the physical handcuffs and leg irons they once wore. Without treatment, the odds are too high that they will end up right back where they started. This is the real threat. This is what must be changed. And this is why I started Lisa Forbes Inc.

Please join me in the fight to return tens of millions of "ex-cons" and "former felons" in America to the point where they can reenter society as restored citizens, where they can turn around and say with gratitude and dignity, "Thank you for your help. I can take it from here."

ACKNOWLEDGMENTS

This book was hard to write and would not be possible without the unconditional support of so many people. I can only name a few of you, but you all know who you are.

Thank you, Risha Grant and Alaina Jones of Risha Grant LLC. You both were foundational in helping me develop the courage to create a public, empowered voice for what had previously been private, painful thoughts and unspoken ideas.

Thank you, Joseph Opala, an anthropologist and former history professor whose lifelong work has been to restore Bunce Island in Sierra Leone. You befriended and educated me as I searched for my African ancestry. I'll never forget how astounded you were to learn just a few details of my life, and how strongly you insisted that this book be written and that my vision be shared. Thank you for reaching out to your friends and asking them to help me write my story.

Thank you, William Paul Davis, a Pulitzer Prize-nominated journalist who helped launch the Historical Writers of America. You answered Joe's calls for help for me and became my "book coach" and also my friend. You were invaluable in asking me questions that forced me to clarify both my story and my intention for sharing it.

Thank you, Jennifer Thompson of Nordlyset Literary Agency. You kept the faith for a very long time that my book would be picked up by the perfect publisher when the time was right. I want to thank the late Eric Huurre, a filmmaker whose award-winning feature documentary, *OPERATION: Emotional Freedom — The Answer*, is a film about PTSD and the effectiveness of energy-based therapies like EFT when used by veterans. I asked Eric to collaborate with me and make a similar documentary that focused on the communities of restored citizens and of Black

Americans. He enthusiastically answered "Yes!" but succumbed to undiagnosed cancer as we were about to begin the project. Eric, I miss you.

And last but not least, thank you, Mercedes Bankston, for being my daughter and my reason for living through all the pain.

Steerforth Press
Truth to Power Books

STEER FORTH PRESS

TRUTH TO POWER

HOW FREE SPEECH SAVED DEMOCRACY

The Untold History of How the First Amendment Became an Essential Tool for Securing Liberty and Social Justice

Christopher M. Finan
Executive Director of the National Coalition Against Censorship
FOREWORD BY RANDALL KENNEDY

"A gripping, moving tale."
— EVAN THOMAS, AUTHOR OF *IKE'S BLUFF*

TRUTH TO POWER

IKE'S MYSTERY MAN
THE SECRET LIVES OF ROBERT CUTLER

The Cold War, the Lavender Scare, and the Untold Story of Eisenhower's First National Security Advisor

PETER SHINKLE

FOREWORD BY
CHARLES KAISER

THE WOMAN WHO INSPIRED AN AFRICAN #METOO MOVEMENT

TOUFAH

Toufah Jallow
with Kim Pittaway

T2P BOOKS // TRUTHFUL NARRATIVES = BETTER UNDERSTANDING

"Hope finds a prominent presence in what so many think is a hopeless, endless conflict."
— *KIRKUS*

NATIONAL JEWISH BOOK AWARDS FINALIST

FRIENDLY FIRE
A MEMOIR

How Israel Became Its Own Worst Enemy and the Hope for Its Future

AMI AYALON

WITH
ANTHONY DAVID

INTRODUCTION BY
DENNIS ROSS

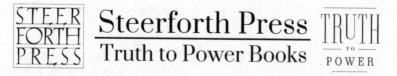

Steerforth Press
Truth to Power Books

STEER FORTH PRESS

TRUTH TO POWER

"A book that is both a history and a sports classic." — *DETROIT FREE PRESS*

"One of the most compelling sports biographies [ever]. A must-read." — *(starred review) BOOKLIST*

HARD DRIVING
THE WENDELL SCOTT STORY

The American Odyssey of
NASCAR's First Black Driver

BRIAN DONOVAN

FOREWORD BY
JOE POSNANSKI

"[A] nuanced, open-minded, de-politicized discussion of our post-#MeToo world." — *REFINERY29*

HAD IT COMING

Rape Culture Meets #MeToo:
Now What?

ROBYN DOOLITTLE

"A must read for nonhistorians seeking a firm
grasp of accurate American history."
— *KIRKUS REVIEWS*

A TRUE HISTORY OF THE UNITED STATES

Indigenous Genocide, Racialized Slavery,
Hyper-Capitalism, Militarist Imperialism,
and Other Overlooked Aspects
of American Exceptionalism

DANIEL A. SJURSEN

"This moving and sprightly book is filled with backstories from America's struggle for
religious freedom that I'll bet you have never heard before . . . a brilliant scholar's
telling insights on the right way for church, state, and society to interact."
— *E.J. DIONNE JR., AUTHOR OF CODE RED AND WHY THE RIGHT WENT WRONG*

SOLEMN REVERENCE

THE SEPARATION OF CHURCH
AND STATE IN AMERICAN LIFE

RANDALL BALMER

Steerforth Press
Truth to Power Books

TRUTH
TO
POWER

T2P BOOKS // TRUTHFUL NARRATIVES = BETTER UNDERSTANDING

"Margaret Kimberley gives us an intellectual gem of prophetic fire about all the US presidents and their deep roots in the vicious legacy of white supremacy and predatory capitalism. Such truths seem more than most Americans can bear, though we ignore her words at our own peril!"
—CORNEL WEST, AUTHOR OF *RACE MATTERS*

PREJUDENTIAL

BLACK AMERICA
AND THE PRESIDENTS

MARGARET KIMBERLEY

T2P BOOKS // TRUTHFUL NARRATIVES = BETTER UNDERSTANDING

"Investigative journalism at its relentless and compassionate best." —KIRKUS REVIEWS
"Methamphetamine was a huge part of this case... A horrible murder driven by drugs."
—PROSECUTOR CAL RERUCHA
"A gripping read." —PEOPLE MAGAZINE

THE BOOK OF MATT

THE REAL STORY OF THE MURDER
OF MATTHEW SHEPARD

STEPHEN JIMENEZ

NEW INTRODUCTION BY
ANDREW SULLIVAN

T2P BOOKS // TRUTHFUL NARRATIVES = BETTER UNDERSTANDING

"This short, powerful book should be required reading for anyone who has ever wondered what it's like to be an ordinary citizen living in a war zone." — *PUBLISHERS WEEKLY*

WHEN THE BULBUL STOPPED SINGING

LIFE IN PALESTINE DURING
AN ISRAELI SIEGE

RAJA SHEHADEH

NEW INTRODUCTION BY
COLUM McCANN

T2P BOOKS // TRUTHFUL NARRATIVES = BETTER UNDERSTANDING

One of three books people "should read to understand what happened in Vietnam."
—THE MARINE CORPS GAZETTE

WAR OF NUMBERS

AN INTELLIGENCE MEMOIR OF THE
VIETNAM WAR'S UNCOUNTED ENEMY

SAM ADAMS

FOREWORD BY
COL. DAVID HACKWORTH

NEW INTRODUCTION BY
JOHN PRADOS

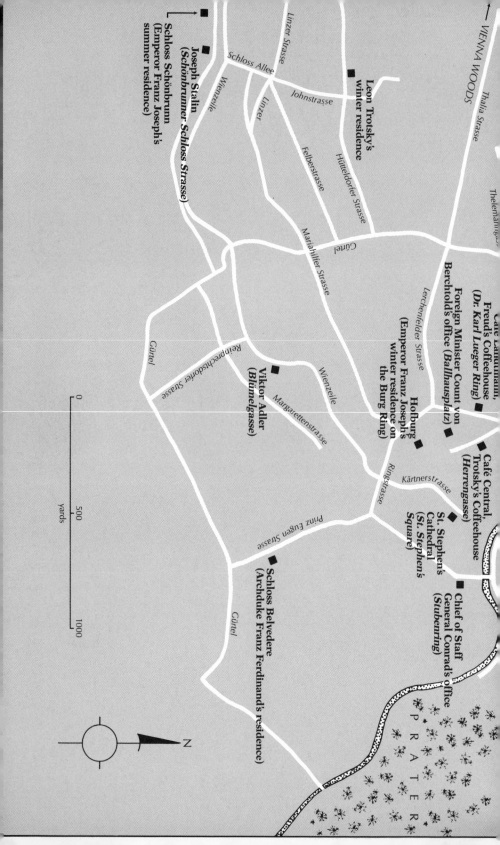

Joseph Stalin
(Schönbrunner Schloss Strasse)

Schloss Schönbrunn
(Emperor Franz Joseph's
summer residence)

Leon Trotsky's
winter residence

Linzer Strasse

Schloss Allee

Johnstrasse

Wienzeile

Linzer

Felberstrasse

Hütteldorfer Strasse

VIENNA WOODS

Thalia Strasse

Thelemanngasse

Mariahilfer Strasse

Gürtel

Gürtel

Reinprechtsdorfer Strasse

Viktor Adler
(Blümelgasse)

Margarettenstrasse

Wienzeile

Lerchenfelder Strasse

Foreign Minister Count von
Berchtold's office (Ballhausplatz)

Hofburg
(Emperor Franz Joseph's
winter residence on
the Burg Ring)

Café Landtmann,
Freud's Coffeehouse
(Dr. Karl Lueger Ring)

Café Central,
Trotsky's Coffeehouse
(Herrengasse)

Kärtnerstrasse

Ringstrasse

Prinz Eugen Strasse

St. Stephen's
Cathedral
(St. Stephen's
Square)

Chief of Staff
General Conrad's Office
(Stubenring)

Gürtel

Schloss Belvedere
(Archduke Franz Ferdinand's
residence)

PRATER

N

0

500

1000

yards